W9-CDS-445

COMPUTER BIBLE STUDY

COMPUTER BIBLE STUDY

Up-to-Date Information on the
Best Software and Techniques

JEFFREY HSU

with

Kermit A. Ecklebarger
Terri A. Gibbs

CONTRIBUTING EDITORS

WORD PUBLISHING
Dallas•London•Vancouver•Melbourne

COMPUTER BIBLE STUDY

Copyright© 1993 by Jeffrey Hsu. All rights reserved. No portion of this book may be reproduced in any form whatsoever, except for brief quotations in reviews, without written permission from the publisher.

Scripture portions quoted from the *Holy Bible, New King James Version,* (NKJV) copyright © 1979, 1980, 1982 by Thomas Nelson, Inc., Publishers, are used by permission.

Those identified as KJV are from the *King James Version* of the Bible.

Those identified as NRSV are from the *New Revised Standard Version* of the Bible, copyright © 1989, by the Division of Christian Education of the National Council of the Churches of Christ USA, and are used by permission.

Those identified as NCV are from *The Holy Bible, New Century Version* copyright Word, Publishing © 1987, 1988, 1991 and are used by persmission.

Library of Congress Cataloging-in-Publication Data:

Hsu, Jeffrey.
    Computer Bible study/Jeff Hsu; with Kermit A. Ecklebarger, Terri A. Gibbs, contributing editors.
        p. cm.
    Includes bibliographical references.
    ISBN 0–8499–3372–2
    1. Bible—Study and teaching—Data processing. 2. Bible—Study and teaching—Automation. I. Ecklebarger, Kermit Allen, 1935– . II. Gibbs, Terri A. III. Title.
    BS600.2.H78   1993
    220'.0285'5—dc20   93–34542
                                           CIP

2 3 4 5 9 XXX 7 6 5 4 3 2 1
Printed in the United States of America

Table of Contents

Preface

While the computer revolution has typically moved at a fantastic pace, it seems that for the past few years Bible computing has progressed even faster!

The idea for this book came two years ago when I began to realize that in spite of the tremendous advances that had been made in computer Bible study products, most Christians were still studying the Bible the way their parents and grandparents had studied it, with printed Bibles, concordances, and reference books—a slow, painstaking task that was as tedious in some ways as it was exciting in others.

In spite of the fact that many of these people had a personal computer or had access to one in their churches or at work, they had never considered the usefulness of the computer for doing Bible study. So it seemed that a book on how to do computer Bible study needed to be written. I have endeavored to write that book and I hope it will prove to be a voyage of discovery for you—a journey spent exploring an entirely new way to study the Bible.

My goal in writing the book is to give you the opportunity to consider a wide variety of programs that are currently on the market, ranging from modest, home-oriented packages to high-powered advanced Bible study systems. I have included chapters that will outline computer techniques, as well as chapters that present the features and benefits of computerized Bible software. Other chapters discuss a range of Bible study methods to help you explore God's Word through the exciting process of electronic computing.

This preface wouldn't be complete without the acknowledgements, which are always a pleasure for me since they come at the end of a long process of thinking, planning, researching, and writing. The path from idea to finished book is never an easy one, and I have been blessed by the kindness and generosity of many who have helped me through this journey.

First on this list is Reverend Jeff Briden, M. Div., who through countless hours of interaction made the Bible come alive to me in a way I had never experienced before. Whether in the broad sweep of the entire Bible, or in the fine details on Bible translations and

Preface

texts, he was instrumental in providing me with the Bible knowledge to write this book. I would also like to thank Dr. Kermit Ecklebarger, of Denver Seminary, for his input on methods of Bible study.

Thanks also go to Doug Brown and Luc VanWorkum for reviewing my original proposal; to my father, Henry Hsu, for reading drafts of my chapters; and to Pastor David Gardiner for suggesting that "the time is right for a book on computerized Bible study."

At Word, Inc., I wish to thank Terri Gibbs, Academic Editor, for a first-class job on making the manuscript the best it can be, and David Pigg, Manager of Academic and Professional Books, for his encouragment throughout the project.

Last, but certainly not least, I thank the Lord, who has provided me with not only the skills and the abilities but also the desire and interest to write about this new revolution in Bible study.

I hope you enjoy the journey!

Jeff Hsu
July 1, 1993

Introduction

This book was developed as a guide to the fascinating and exciting world of computerized Bible study. It includes a comprehensive coverage of all the major types of computerized Bible programs, as well as chapters on related products such as specialized CD-ROM Bible reference libraries, multilingual word processors, Greek/Hebrew study aids, online information, and recreational programs. An important part of the book is Part III with chapters that highlight specific methods of Bible study and show how the computer can make these studies more meaningful and productive.

The chapters in this book are divided into three parts. These are as follows:

Part I — **Basics of Biblical Computing**. The three chapters in Part I, which provide an overview to Bible computing, include information on hardware and software. One chapter also explains basic computer processes.

Part II — **Examining Bible Computing Resources**. There are six chapters in Part II presenting more detailed facts and procedures for a variety of computer resources that relate directly to Bible study. Some of the resources include computerized Bible concordance programs, Greek and Hebrew tools, multilingual word processors, and CD-ROM Bible reference libraries.

Part III — **Applying Computer Technology to Bible Study**. This final section focuses on applying computer programs and processes to four methods of Bible study: word study, biographical study, historical-geographical study, and topical study.

To bring the book to a close, a reference list of software packages that serve as Bible study tools is provided. Information for each package includes the name and address of the manufacturer/distributor, system requirements, Bible versions that are available, Bible resources that are available, and summary comments.

Following is a brief description of each chapter in the book:

Chapter one, **Digital Deuteronomy**, provides advice on how to get started with computerized Bibles. This introduction explains what electronic Bibles are, why they are useful, what they can do, and their advantages and disadvantages. It discusses the benefits of studying with computerized Bibles as opposed to more manual study methods with printed Bibles and resources that are not as efficient and are much more time consuming.

Chapter two, **Chips, Bits, and Bytes**, includes general information on computer hardware and software, particularly as these relate to computerized Bible study. It answers questions such as, What are microprocessors, memory, and modems? and What kind of computer power do I need to do computerized Bible study? The chapter also suggests how to make wise purchases of computer equipment and software programs by evaluating one's needs before buying.

Chapter three, **Electronic Bibles**, is an in-depth look at the features a computerized Bible provides and how associated programs, such as computerized concordances, Greek and Hebrew study aids, and lexicons can help in Bible studies. This chapter serves as an introduction to the chapters on the more specific types of Bible software discussed in Part II.

Chapter four, **Parsing with Programs**, describes the use of the Greek and Hebrew language facilities that are available both in computerized Bible/concordance programs, as well as other related programs. It discusses the advanced Greek/Hebrew features of computerized Bible programs, software that teaches Greek and Hebrew, and the availability of original Greek and Hebrew texts.

Chapter five, **The Tower of Babel on a Disk**, focuses on the use of multilingual word processors to create better sermons, lessons, and notes. It looks at these powerful word processors that offer the ability to work with, display, and print Greek and Hebrew, as well as other languages.

Chapter six, **The Electronic Sermon**, examines the computerized resources that have been developed to help pastors and Bible teachers create better sermons and lessons. This includes databases of Bible illustrations, lesson planners, research aids, and programs for integrating sermons with music.

Chapter seven, **Library on a Disk**, surveys the CD-ROM products available on the market. These small disks provide a massive Bible reference library that can be read, searched, and studied. CD-ROM products provide a wealth of material including multiple English Bible versions, Greek and Hebrew texts, concordances, entire volumes of Bible commentaries, Greek lexicons, Bible dictionaries, wordbooks, sermon illustrations, as well as maps, charts, and graphics.

Chapter eight, **Dialing for Daniel**, considers the wealth of information that is available through a modem and online services. A brief overview of telecommunications is followed by a survey of the vast amount of religion-oriented information that is available through various online services.

Chapter nine, **Not for Kids Only**, presents information on the wide range of educational and recreational Bible software that is accessible today. These computer programs include Bible adventure games, stories from the Bible, Bible paint and color activities, and simulations of Bible stories.

Chapter ten, **Biblical Bytes**, introduces the reader to the Bible study methods that are presented in the next four chapters. Here, each method is discussed briefly along with a guide to the system of presentation that is used in subsequent chapters.

Chapter eleven, **Working with Words**, not only explains how to do Bible word studies on the computer, but also how to organize the information into manageable units for lessons or sermons. The second half of the chapter guides the reader through a sample word study.

Chapter twelve, **Bible Biographies**, explores the intriguing insights that can be gained from studying the lives of people in the Bible. The chapter emphasizes not only how to gather the information by means of computer programs but also how to use the computer to help organize the information. A sample biographic study brings the chapter to a close.

Chapter thirteen, **From Eden to Patmos**, explains how to do a historical-geographical study of a portion of Scripture with the ease of computerized Bible resources. Suggestions are given for organizing the facts and using them in lessons and personal application. Again, samples of historical-geographical studies are included.

Chapter fourteen, **In Touch with Topics**, is an introduction to the topical method of Bible study from the aspect of computerized Bibles. Here again, the method of study and how to organize the results of the study are discussed, followed by an actual topical study.

Finally, a reference list of computer software provides valuable information for acquiring Bible study programs. The information is arranged according to product name for easy reference.

PART I

Basics of Biblical Computing

Chapter One

Digital Deuteronomy:
Exploring the World of Bible Software

> *"God's word is alive and working and is sharper than a double-edged sword."*
> *Hebrews 4:12 NCV*

I f Moses were to bring the ten commandments down from the mountain today, he probably would not carry stone tablets. Instead, he might carry a portable laptop computer and a handful of floppy disks. There would be no thunder, lightning, or trumpets, but, rather, an electronic mail network. Gone are the days of scrolls, quills, and ink pots. Even manual typewriters have all but faded from memory, and their electronic replacements are probably not far behind.

Today, computers, disks, CD-ROMs, and online communication networks are rapidly becoming the indispensable tools for theological research and Bible study. In the past few years, the phenomenal proliferation of computerized Bibles and related programs in the market has revolutionized Bible study. Never before has there been such a wealth of computer-based materials for studying the Bible—whether it be electronic (computerized) Bibles, concordance programs, Greek and Hebrew language software, or CD-ROM databases.

Vendors such as Parsons Technology, Biblesoft, Logos, Bible Research Systems, and others have produced dozens of packages for various computer systems. And major publishers such as Word, Zondervan, NavPress, and others, have devoted considerable effort and resources to developing state-of-the-art biblical software. Continuing improvements and enhancements have resulted in software today that is vastly improved over biblical software sold just a few years ago.

There are many benefits to using a computer for Bible study including (1) the ability to display a passage in different Bible translations concurrently, (2) the ability to find and display specified verses or passages, and (3) the ability to perform sophisticated searches of words, topics, and synonyms. Depending on the specific program used, it is also possible (4) to use Strong's computerized Greek and Hebrew Concordances, (5) to transfer Bible verses and passages to a word processor, (6) to attach notes to particular verses, and (7) to have a complete Bible reference library on one small compact disk (CD). Other resources such as Bible dictionaries, encyclopedias, commentaries, and atlases are also available in computerized form.

Studying the Bible on a computer is an exhilarating experience. Not only do the speed, efficiency, and versatility of computer-based study aids save time and energy, but the wealth of information these programs provide and the intricate functions they perform can almost make a scholar out of even a novice computer operator. In this chapter we will discuss Bible study software in general and will explain why these tools are useful, what functions they can perform, and how they can greatly improve the quality of biblical studies. In the following two chapters we will discuss computer terms and concepts ("Chips, Bits, and Bytes") as well as the specific functions that Bible software can perform ("Electronic Bibles").

Bible Study Software: An Overview

With a computer you can study the Scriptures as never before. In fact:

- You can know exactly where any word you specify in the Bible is located, and you can have a list of all the verses in the Bible where that word occurs.

- In a matter of seconds you can have at your fingertips the Old Testament in Hebrew or the New Testament in Greek with complete parsing on every word.

- With multilanguage programs you can type and print documents using Hebrew or Greek letters.

- You can call a telecommunications computer service and receive current news bulletins and developments from biblical scholars around the world.

- You can ask a theological question on a telecommunications program, and an answer, retrieved from a database of hundreds of volumes, will be transmitted to your screen in seconds.

These are only a few of the truly amazing ways in which computers have changed Bible study and research forever. To guide you through the myriad programs and functions that are available, in the following pages we will briefly overview the various types of computer Bible-study products you can choose from.

Computerized Bibles

The term *computerized* refers to an electronic format as opposed to a printed format. These computer programs usually come complete with various Bible versions or translations and additional Bible study resources. These packages provide immediate and versatile access to the entire Bible text. Not only can the selected text be displayed on the screen or printed out, but these programs allow for interaction with the text and with various translations of the text, which can be viewed side by side on the screen in different windows. Each software package provides the option of unique features and capabilities such as searching the text for a specific word, phrase, or expression, and even creating complex search terms using Boolean (AND, OR) operators. (Boolean operators are explained in detail in chapter three.)

Computerized Concordances

Like their printed counterparts, computer concordances can be used to find the original Hebrew, Greek, or Aramaic word or words

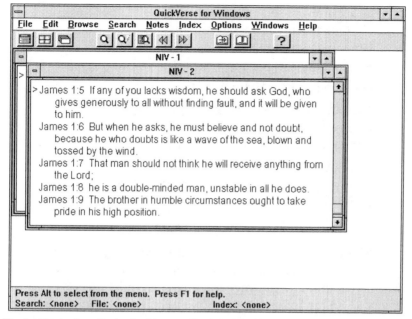

Fig. 1.1 Verses from the book of James. (Courtesy of Parsons Technology.)

upon which any specified English (Bible) word is based. These concordances also indicate all the verses where the word occurs in the Bible. This etymological information is essential to understand correctly the meaning of the Scriptures. The most widely used concordance is Strong's *Concordance*, which is based on the King James Version of the Bible. Concordances for other versions such as the New International Version (NIV) are also available. Since the program does the actual searching, a computerized concordance is timesaving and efficient; it eliminates the need to search for hours through page after page in a printed book. An added bonus is the large, readable text of many electronic versions—a welcome improvement over the tiny letters used in printed concordances.

Bible Encyclopedias and Dictionaries

These helpful computer resources provide general information on a wide range of Bible topics and subjects. Providing detailed and often lengthy expositions of information (sometimes more than a page in length), these tools offer an overview of a particular subject and suggest options for further research.

Bible Atlases

These electronic representations of printed atlases demonstrate graphically the lands and places of the Bible both in the present and in the past. Some of these atlases relate to a specific period in biblical history or to a certain book or passage.

Bible Commentaries

Computer commentaries, like printed commentaries, are biblical reference tools that provide analyses and commentaries on verses, chapters, and books of the Bible. The wealth of information in these computer resources is easily accessed by a few simple keystrokes on the computer.

Greek and Hebrew Language Tools

A wide variety of computer programs are available in this general category. Some of the programs are designed to be used in learning biblical Greek and Hebrew, and others are designed for studying and interacting with the actual Greek or Hebrew text. Original Greek and Hebrew texts are also available that can be used in ways similar to the English Bible versions. The Bible language programs that are available vary from a basic introductory level to advanced programs for scholars who specialize in biblical language studies.

Multilingual Word Processors

These are specialized editor programs that enable the user to create, edit, and modify documents in languages other than English. They generally include foreign language fonts (Hebrew, Greek, Aramaic) that can be displayed onscreen and printed out.

Sermon Preparation Resources

Without doubt these are some of the most helpful programs available for pastors, teachers, and speakers. Designed to assist in preparing intriguing sermons, lessons, or addresses, these programs provide hundreds of timely illustrations and anecdotes; they provide guidelines for organizing and preparing effective sermons and speeches; and they suggest how to effectively integrate music with the material that is presented.

CD-ROM based products

A vast collection of Bible information can be accessed on a CD-ROM disk. One of these small disks stores dozens of biblical reference volumes. CD-ROM products also include multimedia materials that combine advanced graphics, sound, and animation features.

Online Christian Information

With a modem, Bible students today can obtain detailed and current information simply by dialing into one of various telecommunications computer networks. This information includes news services, bibliographic databases, and Christian bulletin boards.

Educational and Recreational Software

The products that are available for the lighter side of Bible study include educational games, tutorial software, as well as recreational software that transports the user back in time to relive and interact with people, places, and situations from Bible days.

The Advantages and Disadvantages of Computer Bible Study

Computer programs have opened up a whole new world of capabilities and possibilities for people who are interested in studying the Bible. Just a few years ago, the vast wealth of information available with a computer was limited to highly trained Bible scholars. And although the advancements have been significant, they are just the beginning of developments in the computer industry that are likely to continue expanding at dizzying speeds in the foreseeable future.

Computer Bible study offers many advantages, to be sure, but admittedly there are also some disadvantages to this process.

To be honest and realistic, we need to consider both the advantages and the disadvantages.

Advantages

Efficiency. One of the greatest advantages of the computer is that it *saves time!* Through this powerful mechanism it is possible to look up verses, move back and forth through various passages in the Bible, search for words or phrases, and print out long texts (in either English, Greek, or Hebrew) in a matter of seconds—a fraction of the time these same functions would require working manually with the printed form.

Versatility. Not only is the computer timesaving, it is also versatile! A greater variety of tasks can be completed in far less time than without a computer. For example, multiple Bible translations can be studied simultaneously, biblical language data can be utilized, electronic notes can be attached to verses for further reference, and texts from selected Bible versions can be transferred to a computer "note pad" to be stored or printed out.

Dexterity. Some things can be done on the computer that would be virtually impossible under the constraints of human mental and physical capabilities. Consider, for example, that a computer can search for phrases throughout the Bible (extremely difficult to do even with a concordance) but can also search for an incomplete phrase when only one or two of the correct words in the phrase is known. In fact, it can search for a variety of possible combinations of words in the phrase. Also, some programs cross-reference their computerized Bible study tools, which means that related references can be found in several different sources without ever reentering the topic or verse.

Variety. The capabilities of Bible-related software far surpass traditional Bible study tools not only in dexterity but also in variety. Whether interested in scholarly, general, or recreational Bible activities, there is a computer program designed to interest everyone.

Integration. With a computer, the difficulties of working at a desk cluttered with Bible translations, concordances, lexicons, Bible encyclopedias, and numerous other books can be a thing of the past. Bible software is designed precisely so that multiple interrelated tools can be accessed quickly from one program screen and can function in coordination with each other.

Disadvantages

A basic knowledge of computer operation is necessary. As obvious as it may seem, in order to study the Bible by computer it is necessary to have at least a rudimentary knowledge of how computers and software programs operate. This information is not difficult to obtain or to understand, but it is a prerequisite to successful computer Bible study.

Unique instructions must be learned for each program. Depending on the software, Bible study programs can range from simple to extremely complicated. While most programs are set up so that basic functions can be learned relatively quickly, they may also have advanced features that require extensive time to learn to use properly.

The power of the computer must be adequate for the program. Bible programs work with large amounts of data that require sufficient computer power to operate. While many programs will work with the limited power that is available with the majority of computers on the market today, most of the more complex programs require computers with increased power capabilities. (Further details on computer hardware and performances are provided in the chapter "Chips, Bits, and Bytes.")

Program functions may be limited without a hard drive. Consider the size of the Bible, then multiply that by several versions. Add to this the space needed to hold the Strong's *Concordance,* Greek and Hebrew texts, and computerized resources such as Bible dictionaries and it is easy to see why a large hard disk with abundant storage is best for serious Bible study. Indeed, some of the more elaborate programs themselves require as much as 15 megabytes of disk space. Obviously, while it is not necessary to have a hard disk to do computer Bible study, the functions that can be performed using only floppy disks are limited.

Computer programs are subject to computer problems. Files can be lost, the hard disk can "crash," and programs can malfunction. Although these difficulties are generally infrequent, they do happen. Anyone who wants to study with computer programs needs to be aware of these possibilities and needs to know how to handle them.

In Closing

In brief, this is the world of computer Bible study! It is a whole new realm of advanced capabilities that could revolutionize the way you study the Bible. With the simple click of a switch you can study efficiently and effectively, in more ways and in less time than you ever dreamed possible.

But in order to work successfully with computers and programs, it is helpful to have a basic knowledge of their pieces and parts and how they operate. So in the next chapter we will discuss the basic components of computers and disks. We will describe briefly how each functions and what it contributes to the efficiency of the computing process. This will enable you to:

1. understand the features of Bible computer programs that are discussed in this book,

2. make informed Bible software purchases,

3. be able to operate and interact with the programs you purchase.

Now, your adventure begins!

Chapter Two

Chips, Bits, and Bytes:
Computer Systems and Software for Bible Study

> *"Open my eyes to see the miracles in your teachings."*
> *Psalm 119:18 (NCV)*

I f you don't have a computer, it probably won't be long until you do. The field of computers and computer programming is expanding almost faster than we can keep up with it, and there is no end in sight! Dozens of biblical software packages are on the market, from home-oriented programs to advanced Bible study resources for pastors and theological scholars. Whether your goals are to enhance your personal Bible studies and devotions, to prepare a Sunday school lesson or a sermon, or to research detailed theological issues, there are resources available to help you.

Computerized Bible study can bring rich rewards; however, they are rewards that cannot be enjoyed without some effort—not only in learning how to utilize each program, but in developing a general familiarity with how computers function. If you are already knowledgeable about computers, you may want to move ahead to the next chapter. For those who are moving into unchartered waters, the following pages will provide sufficient information for a brief working knowledge of the computer.

If you are in the market for a computer, it will be helpful to understand these basic concepts so you will know what kind of hardware and equipment are necessary to use Bible programs effectively. You will know whether you need a hard disk, and if so, what size and what kind. You will know about the speed of your processor and the necessity of add-ons such as modems, CD-ROM drives, and printers.

In addition, while most programs require only a minimum of computer knowledge, being familiar with computer terms, concepts, and functions will facilitate the entire computing process. Understanding some computer jargon will allow you to read the program manual and understand the instructions clearly. It will also enable you to move on to more advanced functions in the program and will alert you to errors that need to be avoided. In short, it will ensure enjoyable study with a minimum of frustration, headaches, and disappointments.

Computer Systems and Bible Software

The two basic terms to understand in computing are *hardware* and *software*. Hardware is the physical computer machinery that runs the programs, prints out text, and displays images to the screen among numerous other tasks. Hardware includes the computer unit, a monitor (screen), a printer, and add-ons such as a modem. The software, also known as the *computer program*, provides the instructions that tell the computer what to do. A computer software program is sometimes referred to as a "package" since many individual programs make up the complete unit.

Bible software, or programs, consist of two basic parts: large electronic databases (collections) of information and associated materials, and a set of instructions used to work with the data. Thus, Bible programs that are text-oriented contain an enormous amount of data in addition to various sets of instructions for working with the text.

Computer programs, or software, are interactive with the other part of the computing process—the hardware. Each program has a distinct set of system requirements, that is, the minimum hardware necessary for the program to function properly. The most significant requirements that each program takes into consideration are:

- type and speed of processor
- type of operating system (DOS or Windows)
- amount of usable memory
- size of hard disk
- type of video card and display
- available peripherals

In order to understand why these elements are crucial for computer programming, we will briefly overview how each one functions in the computing process.

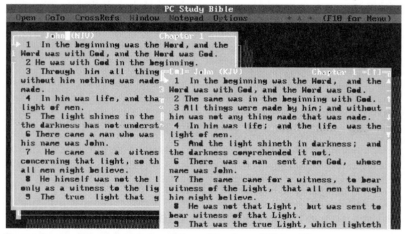

Fig. 2.1 Screen view of multiple translations. (Courtesy of Biblesoft.)

The Components of Computing

The Microprocessor

The computer's microprocessor (sometimes known as its CPU or Central Processing Unit) functions as the brain of the computer system. It makes all the necessary calculations and moves data back and forth between the different parts of the system. Without doubt this is the most important part of the computer, since it does most of the work required to run programs.

Most IBM-PC and compatible computers are based on the Intel family of microprocessors, which originally were designated as the 8086 and 8088. While subsequent models included the 80286 and 80386, today the most powerful models are the 80486 and Pentium™ chips. Frequently, the more advanced microprocessors (80286 and higher) are referred to simply by their last three digits, such as 286, 386, or 486. Each level in the hierarchy of microprocessors provides greater speed in performing processor commands, increased computing capabilities, and additional advanced features.

A subject of continuing discussion is the question of how fast a processor is really necessary, especially when there is such a variety to choose from. It is difficult to provide a definitive answer to this question, but in the case of computerized Bible study, it is generally advisable for you to have as fast a processor as you can reasonably afford. The reasons for this are twofold: (1) Bible study programs run more efficiently with a fast processor, and (2) it is very likely that as the power and sophistication of such programs improve, they will ultimately require faster processors anyway.

If you do not have a computer yet, it is a good idea to determine what software you want to work with before you buy a computer. This will assure that you have sufficient power to use the software of your choice.

Another feature of microprocessors that must be considered is the clock speed, measured in megahertz (MHz), or millions of cycles per second. The clock speed, or how many times the microprocessor's clock crystal vibrates per second, is a measure of the speed at which the computer will perform commands. Early microcomputers, such as the original IBM-PC, operated at a clock speed of 4.77 MHz, while current systems offer clock speeds as fast as 25, 33, 50, and even 66 MHz. In some cases a microprocessor is manufactured in various clock speeds, so if there is not a large difference in price, it is always advisable to select a processor with a fast clock speed.

Generally, the processor type is mentioned with its clock speed, such as 386DX-25 or 386DX-33 or 486DX-50. In such cases, the processor type is at the left, followed by the dash and the clock speed. Although a faster processor provides a better performance overall, it is not necessary to have the fastest processor, such as a 50 MHz 80486 or the Pentium chip, in order to do computer Bible study. In fact, a processor in the 80386 or 80486 range would be more than adequate.

Operating System

The operating system allows the user to interact with the hardware. All IBM-PC and compatibles function by means of a Disk Operating System (DOS), which is a collection of programs designed to correlate the activities between the hardware and the software. DOS, marketed under the names MS-DOS and PC-DOS, has been one of the most widely used operating systems in recent years. It is basically a command-driven operating system requiring that the user memorize commands and follow strict rules for their use.

Another operating system that is widely used today is Microsoft Windows. This system is based on a graphical user interface (GUI). A GUI operates on a graphical, visual approach to computing rather than a command approach. Thus, the Windows system presents commands, programs, and programming choices by means of symbols, boxes, and pointers. Icons appear on the screen and the user simply points with an electronic "mouse" to the icon representing the command desired and "clicks" the mouse to activate the command. In order to run Microsoft Windows efficiently, a fast processor and a large amount of memory are necessary.

Memory

The memory capabilities of a computer are an important consideration when purchasing either hardware or software. All of the information that is accessed or input into the computer must be held somewhere and, in this case, it is held in the main memory, or RAM (random access memory). The memory of a computer is something like an enormous array of mailboxes, each with its own unique number, or address, and each one capable of holding a certain amount of information. Therefore, the more memory you have available, the larger the programs you can run, and the more information and data you can work with at any one time.

Another kind of memory is used internally by the computer system. These memory chips, known as ROM (Read-Only Memory), are designed to hold system-level programs and routines. Fortunately you do not need to be overly concerned with how much or what kind of ROM is in your computer.

Because many of the more comprehensive Bible software packages work with large amounts of data, it is advisable to have ample RAM memory not only to run the program, but also to allow it to run at a reasonably fast speed. Most programs will specify the amount of memory that is required to run the program, but keep in mind this is usually just the minimum. The more system memory that is available in your computer the more room the operating system will have not only for additional functions but for more efficient processing. Let's face it—the basic reasons for doing Bible study on a computer are to save time and to perform tedious tasks quickly. So you will want to have sufficient memory to make this possible.

Computer memory is measured in terms of thousands of bytes, or kilobytes (K), and in terms of millions of bytes, or megabytes (MB). One byte is roughly equivalent to one character. You really need to have a minimum of 640K (640 kilobytes, or about 640,000 characters) of RAM memory in your DOS-based system, however, extra memory in the neighborhood of 2, 4, or 8 megabytes (millions of bytes) would be even better. You may need to use some form of memory management software to use this expanded and extended memory, but the end result will be better performance and higher speed.

Increasingly, Bible software is being written for Microsoft Windows, which means it is probably wise to have sufficient memory to run Windows efficiently. The best way to determine how much memory you will need in your computer is to investigate the system requirements for the software you wish to run and then to acquire a system that at least meets those requirements. However, as a general rule, it is always best to have more than the minimum requirements of the program, because subsequent add-on programs or updated versions may become more power hungry.

Hard Disk

While the RAM memory of a computer is like a set of mailboxes, each one temporarily holding a limited amount of information, the hard disk of a computer is like a filing cabinet that holds large amounts of data permanently. Most new computers come complete with a hard disk drive already installed. It is an added feature that allows for faster access to programs and data.

Although many Bible programs can be operated without a hard disk, anyone who wants to work with multiple Bible versions and associated study resources will certainly need to have one installed in their computer. Although a simple program with a single Bible translation may not take up much space, a more complex program with several English translations, a Strong's *Concordance*, original Greek and Hebrew texts, and other add-ons can require up to 15, 20, or even more megabytes on a hard disk.

Floppy Disks

Aside from hard disks, another means of permanent storage of information is the floppy disk. This is a small, plastic disk coated with metal oxide in order to hold a magnetic charge. Read-write heads in the floppy disk drive read the magnetic information from the disk and write information onto it for storage. The two main PC diskette formats are the 5¼ inch floppy disk and the 3½ inch (hard case) floppy disk. Both of these disks are produced in low and high density versions, with the 5¼ inch diskette holding 360K (360,000 bytes) and 1.2MB (1,200,000 bytes) of data, and the 3½ inch holding 720K (720,000 bytes) and 1.44MB (1,440,000 bytes) of data. Although the low and high density disks appear to be identical, there is a vast difference between their memory capabilities. The choice of high or low density disk is determined by the low or high density capabilities of the floppy disk drive. Each drive is designed to read one or the other.

While older models of computers were designed only with the 5¼ inch drive, more recent models include both sizes of drives as a standard feature. However, with the increasing popularity of the 3½ inch disk, many of the newest systems are designed with only the 3½ inch disk drive.

In terms of software, many packages provide both sizes of diskettes sold either together in one unit or separately in two versions of the same program. The choice between single or dual floppy drive configurations is entirely a personal preference.

Monitor

A computer monitor is much like a television screen, except that it only displays text and images transmitted by the computer. Affordability is the most basic consideration when buying a monitor, but keep in mind that Bible programs are easier to work with on a large monitor. Since Bible programs display considerable detail on the screen (text, icons, graphics, etc.), and many provide the information in multiple windows, a larger monitor will allow the screens and data to be more readable. If you plan to run a program under Microsoft Windows with high resolution, a large monitor screen display is especially beneficial. For most programs, a monitor with a screen diameter in the neighborhood of fourteen to fifteen inches is a good choice; however, for higher resolutions larger sizes are needed so the text is readable.

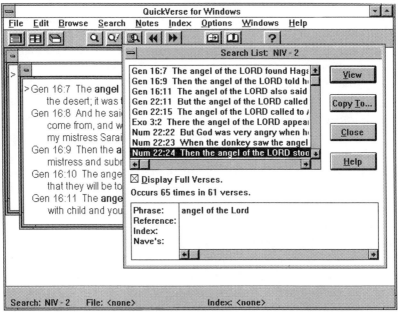

Fig. 2.2 Phrase search of "angel of the Lord." (Courtesy of Parsons Technology.)

Graphics Board

A graphics board is an adapter that controls what is displayed on the screen and how it is displayed. The board is installed in one of the expansion slots of the computer, and cables connect it to the video monitor. Graphics boards vary depending on screen mode and resolution type. This distinction is specified by the letters representing the type, such as Super VGA, EGA, or CGA. Each one of these relates to how many pixels (little dots) are used to compose the images on the screen. The better the resolution, the greater the number of pixels that are used, and thus the sharper the image on the screen. Although it may seem confusing, frequently a specific graphics card (such as a VGA card) can support several different modes, such as CGA and EGA. Each program will specify which card is part of its system requirements.

Many of the new Bible software programs operate best using EGA, VGA, and Super VGA (or other high resolution) modes as these provide clear, detailed, and refined images.

Printer

The printer is actually a separate machine attached to the computer that prepares a hard copy or printout of information accessed from the memory of the computer. Depending upon the capabilities of a particular program, it is possible to print copies of Scripture passages, Bible texts integrated with personal comments, Greek and Hebrew texts, or biblical maps and illustrations.

There are several kinds of printers on the market, including dot matrix, ink jet, and laser. Dot matrix printers form letters and graphics characters by striking tiny metal pins against a ribbon onto the paper. These print text quickly and have the capability to print graphics. While early dot matrix printers produced poor quality letters, new "letter quality" dot matrix, such as those sold as 24 pin, provide very good resolution printing.

Ink jet printers form characters by spraying tiny droplets of ink onto the paper. While they offer high quality resolution, they tend to have print that smears easily.

Laser printers are the most versatile, and they produce high quality resolution. They are ideal for printing text using different fonts and typefaces, for producing high quality graphics, and for reproducing legible Greek and Hebrew text.

For general use, a good quality dot matrix printer is sufficient, but for those interested in having the full range of capabilities, a laser printer is worth the investment.

CD-ROM Drive

A CD-ROM (Compact-Disk Read-Only Memory) drive is a device that uses a laser to read data off of the surface of a small circular platter resembling a music CD. The term "read-only memory" means that information can be read from the disk, but nothing on the disk can be changed. A CD-ROM drive is not a part of most computer systems but can be added to a system. For those interested in advanced Bible study and multimedia, it would provide access to vast libraries of biblical information. Dozens of reference works, thousands of pages long, can be found on CD-ROM programs such as the CDWord Library or The New Bible Library.

Mouse

A mouse is a fairly recent innovation in computer systems. It is a small, input device attached to the computer that is manipulated manually to give commands to the computer. By pointing to icons or objects on the monitor and clicking the mouse button, the user activates the program instructions. Many consider this method of giving commands to the computer much easier and more enjoyable than the standard method of typing in commands from a keyboard. Also, the recent emphasis on graphical user interfaces (GUIs) and windowing (such as Microsoft Windows) has made the mouse increasingly popular in computing circles.

Although a mouse is not required for many DOS programs, the programs can be used more effectively with one. The most common type of mouse can simply be plugged into a port at the back of the computer system, but another type requires the addition of an interface board in one of the computer expansion slots.

Modem

A modem is another add-on device that can translate incoming data from a telephone line into a form of electrical codes that can be read by a computer and vice versa. A modem acts as a mediator making information from the world at large directly accessible through a telephone line to any computer operator. Modems are particularly useful for gaining access to a wide range of current information that is provided by commercial online services, database vendors, and bulletin boards. Special communications software is required for access to these telecommunications features, and, of course, it is necessary to install a modem as well as the specific cables and wiring that connect the modem to the telephone.

Modems are usually priced according to the number of features that are provided and the access speed. As such, prices vary widely. (This will be discussed in further detail in the chapter entitled, "Dialing for Daniel.")

Sound Board

Sound is an expanding area in computing. With the newly developed sound boards, it is now possible to enjoy quality sound in programs beyond the standard speaker beeps and video arcade effects. A sound board is a circuit board that can be added to the computer to expand its sound capabilities. Once it is plugged into a computer expansion slot and hooked up to speakers, it can transform a mundane computer program into a true multi-media experience. Many of the contemporary Bible games come alive in this way, far surpassing the sound capabilities of a standard computer speaker.

A sound card is useful particularly for game and multimedia programs (including those mentioned in this book), however, for most Bible study programs it is not necessary.

Evaluating Your Own Needs

As anyone who has spent time shopping for computer hardware and software knows, choosing what to buy can be complicated and frustrating. There are so many different products on the market, it can be confusing to wade through all the brands, choices, add-ons, and options that are available. Purchasing even a small item can be complicated, and yet it must be done carefully because although there are bargains to be found, computer hardware and software tend to be costly. Purchasing a computer or a software program is definitely a worthwhile investment, but one that must be made wisely.

The first step in making a wise purchase is to consider your needs, both present and future, and to evaluate what computer

Bible study equipment will best meet those needs within the constraints of your budget. A basic rule of thumb to follow is to purchase quality equipment that not only meets your immediate needs and expectations but exceeds them at least somewhat. This will allow you to expand and develop in your studies without making additional purchases. While you do not want to make excessive acquisitions, neither do you want to have equipment that is so bare-bones it is inadequate to meet your needs.

In order to help you make informed and intelligent choices, on the following pages we suggest some questions to ask before deciding which computer product to buy. The questions are organized according to three categories of individuals, from those who are novices with computers or Bible study, to those who are proficient with computers and want to do advanced Bible studies. Use these questions to determine exactly what you want to accomplish and what equipment will help you to accomplish it.

For Personal Bible Study

The first category of users comprise the personal Bible study group. These individuals want to use a computer to enhance their personal Bible studies with electronic Bible study tools.

Since the computer programs that would be appropriate in this category are designed for home and personal use, the main factors to consider are price and a reasonable number of features. To begin with, select a computer Bible study package that you consider "friendly" or easy to use (whether DOS or Windows) and that offers several English Bible translations, a Bible dictionary, and a concordance. (You could consider adding other versions and resources later.) Bible games and recreational packages would also be appropriate for home and personal use.

Here are some basic questions to ask when purchasing personal Bible study software:

System Requirements:

- What are the system requirements of the package you are considering, and what hardware does your machine have? Are the two compatible?

Program:

- Do you want to work with just one Bible translation or with several translations? Does this program include more than one translation? Are other translations planned for the future? Are other translations available as optional add-ons?

- Do you want to have access to the original Greek and Hebrew words? Does the program include a concordance or a similar feature? Is one planned for the future? Is it available as an add-on?

- Does the program offer Greek and Hebrew language texts of the Bible? Are these planned for the future?

- What other resources are available or offered as options that you might be interested in adding later?

- Does the program provide the capabilities you will need for your studies (i.e., searching, printing)?

- Does the program feature mouse support?

- Is the program for DOS or Windows?

- Is the price reasonable for the features of the program?

- Does the program provide a document editor or an easy way to transfer information to a word processor?

- What technical support is available? Does the vendor have an 800 toll free support line? (Technical support may be offered in the form of calls to technical personnel, by support mail, or even through inquiries to a BBS [bulletin board service]. Some vendors provide unlimited support while others provide free support over a certain period of time and after that require a fee. (**This consideration is particularly important for those who are unfamiliar with computer systems.**)

Bible packages vary widely in price. Some of the "shareware" programs, which offer a wide range of features, can be quite reasonable in cost while the widely advertised commercial packages, together with a whole set of optional Bible versions, can be significantly more expensive. If you are concerned about cost, shareware Bible vendors are extremely helpful, and in many cases will allow you to try out the program before buying.

Intermediate Bible Study

This category includes those who are interested in more challenging Bible studies that involve working with the original Greek and Hebrew texts, researching for information in Bible dictionaries and commentaries, and preparing sermons and lessons. Individuals in this category will want to look beyond the most basic programs to consider more sophisticated Bible software packages.

Here are some good questions to consider when looking for intermediate Bible study programs.

System Requirements:

• What are the system requirements of the program? Is this compatible with your equipment? At this level you should expect that the requirements will be greater. They might include a more advanced processor such as a 386 or 486, a fast megahertz speed (25 or higher), ample disk space (10, 20MB or more), and a graphics card of EGA or greater.

Program:

• Does the program offer the features you need for your studies? Are the features insufficient or excessive for your needs?

• Does the program include helps for sermon preparation such as a built-in notepad or editor?

• Can the program work in conjunction with a standard word processor?

• What additional options are available for the program or are being planned for the future?

• What technical support is available?

Advanced Bible Study

Individuals who are involved in advanced Bible study will be interested in the highly specialized Bible programs that are available. In addition to the intermediate programs mentioned above, these individuals would want to consider acquiring lexical and grammatical tools for working with Greek and Hebrew as well as CD-ROM based biblical libraries. Online religious news services, databases, and related resources would also be of interest.

Here are some strategic questions that relate to this high end of computer Bible study:

System Requirements:

- What system requirements are needed? Are they compatible with what is available to you? In addition to a powerful computer and ample memory space, some of the products and services available for advanced Bible study require additional hardware, such as a CD-ROM drive or a modem.

Program:

- What features are available on the program? Will they meet your needs?
- Does the program include several translations and reference works?
- Are technical add-on options available or planned for the future?
- Is good documentation provided for the user?

In Closing

Whatever your level of interest or background in Bible study, the computer can make your studies not only more effective and time-efficient, but more enjoyable too. Computer Bible study is a whole new approach to studying God's Word with advantages that readily convince even the serious skeptics. Now that we have overviewed basic computer equipment, let's move on to explore the things we can actually do in computer Bible study.

Chapter Three

Electronic Bibles:
Basic Computer Processes

*"Let the word of Christ dwell in you
richly in all wisdom."*
Colossians 3:16 *(KJV)*

An assuring note of information from one computer manual states—"No matter what happens, you cannot break the computer!" That encouragement seems like a good basis for an overview of the Bible study and research operations that can be done with computer programs. Computer Bible study programs, like any kind of software, can only be used successfully by learning precisely how to execute the functions that are part of each program and by practicing the instructions of each function in order to master the process. Although these programs may be completely new to you, do not be intimidated by the unknown. Because, on the whole, Bible study programs are easy to use, and although one program may differ from another in the precise functions it can perform and the exact commands and key presses that are necessary to effect those functions, the same basic features are common to most computerized Bible programs.

In this chapter we will briefly discuss the basic procedures that are possible with computer Bible study programs. Our goal is to help you become knowledgeable about what various computer Bible software can do and to encourage you to gain experience in working with these types of programs.

Bible Study Software Capabilities

The main type of Bible study program is the *computerized Bible*. This term refers to a program that allows the user to access and work with Bible translations, original language texts, and associated resources on the computer screen. Sometimes these programs are referred to as electronic Bibles or Bible concordance programs. Computerized Bibles are more widely used than any other kind of Bible software because they provide access to the electronic form of the Bible. Working with this database of text is so much more efficient and precise than working with the printed Bible and various versions that the benefits are obvious. Foremost among these benefits is the simple fact that in working with the electronic form of the Bible, the user is not working alone; the multiple features and capabilities of the program are also working— at amazing speeds and with incredible power.

But exactly how does the computerized Bible help in study and research? Let's look at what can be done with these programs.

Finding and Displaying Text

One of the most fundamental features of Bible software is the ability to find a specified verse or passage of Scripture anywhere in the Bible within seconds. In addition, multiple occurrences of a verse or subject can be found, and the verse or passage can be studied in parallel versions simultaneously.

Finding Text. No longer do you need to search through a table of contents, index, or concordance at the back of your Bible to find a specific verse. You can enter either the reference of the verse (if you know it) or a word or phrase from the verse, and the system will display the actual verse text on your computer screen within seconds. The process is just as simple if you want to find two dozen or so passages scattered throughout both the Old and New Testaments, perhaps while doing a topical study. Again, you simply type in a word or phrase that indicates the topic and the program will display a list of every verse where the subject is mentioned throughout the Bible.

Bible software packages are designed to make the process of finding books, chapters, and verses as easy as possible. In some programs, you simply type in the book or range of verses you want the system to retrieve and display on the screen. For example, you could type in the book of John, you could indicate a range of verses perhaps from John 3:1 to 3:18, or you could ask for just one verse such as John 3:16. In other programs, especially those that run under Microsoft Windows or have their own built-in windowing capabilities, verses or ranges of verses are chosen by means of menus and menus bars (graphic lists of choices that are displayed on the screen).

Whatever the method, using the computer to search and find a specific reference is an important feature of computer Bible programs that will make your study time more efficient and productive.

Displaying Bible Text. After retrieving a specific Bible text, the Bible program will display it on the screen just as it appears in the printed text, usually with its book, chapter, and verse reference. Some programs even highlight Jesus' words on the screen in red just like in a printed Bible. Depending on the program, computerized Bible programs will display text from a certain Bible version or translation in a window thus allowing it to be moved around and resized according to individual needs. Some Bible programs allow generous control of the displayed text including the ability to change the text color, the background color, the color of highlighted text, and the color of Christ's words.

Displaying Multiple Versions. With electronic programs it is possible to view different versions of the Bible simultaneously on the same screen. Do you want to compare a word, verse, or passage in the King James Version (KJV) with one in the New King James Version (NKJV)? Or do you want to compare something in the New American Standard Bible (NASB) with the New International Version (NIV)? Bible computer programs can display identical verses or passages from multiple translations in windows that are side by side on the screen, a feature known as parallel translations. The windows are clearly labeled to identify each translation or version. Some programs present the same verses in two different versions through "linked windows" that track each other as different references are displayed.

Depending on the software package, there are many different versions to choose from. Of course, by investing in multiple packages it is possible to have nearly every version of the Bible available including the original Greek and Hebrew texts.

Bookmarks

A bookmark is a special feature of some packages that allows the user to mark the text at the completion of a period of study in order to pick up from that same spot in the text in a subsequent study session.

Searching

Searching Capabilities. One of the most powerful and important advantages of computer Bible programs is the ability to search through Bible texts (or the entire Bible for that matter) for various words and phrases that can be either highly specific or loosely specified. While it is possible to perform a simple word search by using a printed concordance, a computer Bible program can perform the same search with much greater speed and can provide various options (such as Boolean capabilities) to help increase the power and sophistication of the search.

In some programs it is possible to set the scope of the search, thus restricting it to the Old or New Testament, or to a certain book or chapter. For example, you can search for occurrences of a word or phrase in the entire Bible, just in the Old Testament, just in the New Testament, in the entire book of John, in John chapters 1–10, in John chapter 3, or, being very specific, in John 3:1–3:10.

Single Word Searches. This is the simplest form of searching. The purpose is to discover all the verses in the Bible, or within a specified range of the Bible, that contain a certain word—perhaps the word *prayer* or *love*. Some programs allow for searches not only of English words but also of Greek or Hebrew words.

Phrase Searches. A slightly more complex search, the phrase search locates the occurrences of specific sequences of words. Many Bible phrases such as "day of the Lord" or "seven stars and Orion" have meanings that are not derived from the meaning of each word in the phrase but, rather, are unique to a particular combination of words in a particular context. Understanding the meaning of these phrases is an important part of Bible study. However, while there have been countless studies done on *fear, Lord,* or *redeemer,* there have been far fewer studies completed on "fear of the Lord" or "kinsman-redeemer." With computer program search capabilities, studies such as these are now much more feasible.

In addition, some subjects can only be studied as phrases either because they are not mentioned as a single word or because they are not adequately described by any one word. Consider the example of *homosexuality,* which is certainly a topic of current interest. The word homosexuality is never mentioned in the Bible, but related phrases such as "inordinate affections," "vile affections," and "burning with lust" are.

Advanced Boolean Searches. No, these are not searches for "Booleans," whatever that might be. Rather, they are complex searches for various combinations of words using specific tags or "Boolean operators" (named after George Boole, a founder of modern symbolic logic, the basis for all computer operations). For instance, if you wanted to look for verses that contained both *Jesus* and *prayer,* you could perform this search by using the Boolean tag **AND—Jesus AND Prayer.**

Here is a list of the basic Boolean search operations that can be used.

- ____ **AND** ____ This operator will search for verses that contain the two words indicated.

- ____ **OR** ____ With this operator, verses will be retrieved if either of the words indicated match. For instance, you can find all the verses that contain either the words **divorce OR fornication,** or both.

- ____ **XOR** ____ This operator is called the exclusive OR, and is a variant of the OR operator. When you use this Boolean operation, **divorce XOR fornication,** the computer will search for all the verses that contain either of the words, but not both. Verses that contain both will be deleted from the list.

- ____ **NOT** ____ This is referred to as the negation Boolean and is usually used together with another search word. For example, if you wanted to find the verses that contain the words *Jesus* but not *Christ,* you would indicate the following search: **Jesus NOT Christ.**

Wildcard Searches. Frequently, it is helpful to perform searches based not on just one word, but on all variations of a word. For example, a complete study of *prayer* would need to include other variations of the word such as *pray, prayed, prays, prayer, praying, prayeth,* and so forth. The wildcard capability, in this instance **pray*** (* indicates wildcard), allows you to generalize your search by keeping part of the search term specific and the rest more general. Thus, all verses containing any grammatical form that includes *pray* would be listed. Imagine the hours of time that can be saved with these search capabilities; they eliminate the necessity of doing a separate search for every form or variation of the word.

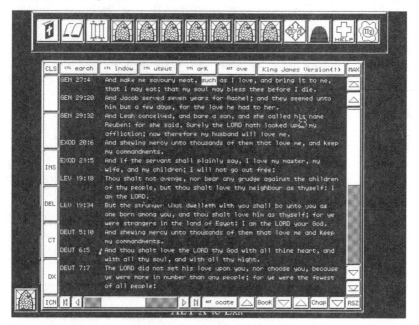

Fig. 3.1 Word search through a computerized Bible. (Courtesy of Word, Inc.)

Complex Searches. By combining various search terms with Boolean operators, it is possible to create multiple types of complex searches according to individual needs. Some programs allow the use of several Boolean operators together in order to create a complex search expression, or the use of parentheses to group certain search terms together. For example the following command—**redeem* NOT redeemer AND (grace OR mercy OR love)**—would search for all the verses with words relating to *redeem,* excluding the word *redeemer,* and also having either the words *grace, mercy,* or *love.*

Search Proximity. Another feature commonly found in computerized Bibles is the search proximity. This feature lets you set boundaries for your searches. Thus, rather than looking for every verse where a word occurs, you can set up a search proximity of four, which means that you want to find the word only in a group of four continuous verses.

Case Sensitivity. The case sensitive search is programmed to search for only the specified case or grammatical designation of a word and for no others. For example, a search for *God* would not include instances of *god*.

Search Spell Checking. If you do not know how to spell the word you want to search for, you can look it up in a list of words or topics. Some programs offer partial word searches, in which case you type in the first few letters of the word and a list of words with those initial letters will appear on the screen.

Count of Found Verses. When you execute a search, many programs will indicate how many verses were found for that search term. With this list you can then decide whether to actually view the verses or to narrow the search to selected verses.

For example, you can start with a very large topic, such as the word *God*. A study of this word in the entire Bible (KJV) will reveal a whopping 3,875 verses. Even if you choose to break this down into the Old Testament (2,687 verses) or the New Testament (1,188 verses), you will still have a large amount of material to work with. A simpler approach is to restrict the scope of the study even further, perhaps to the Prophets in the Old Testament (Isaiah through Malachi). This would reduce the number of verses to 661. It would be even more manageable to study the word *God* only in the book of Isaiah; there you would have to deal with about 123 verses. Limiting the scope of a search can help to make a study more manageable.

Searches by Strong's Number. Another way to search for a Bible text is to use the number system from Strong's *Concordance*. This volume lists almost every Greek and Hebrew word in the Bible (KJV) by number and indicates where they are found. If you have a computerized Strong's *Concordance,* you can quickly search for all the verses that use a particular Greek or Hebrew word. For example, the word *agapē* (love) is designated by the number 26 and the word *phileō* (love) is designated by 5368. By completing a comparative study of these two words you would be able to understand more accurately the biblical meaning of love.

Writing and Editing

An important part of any computerized Bible program is the ability to extract, copy, and work with the Bible text. This is one of the basic advantages to working with an electronic Bible rather than a printed Bible.

Editor. Computerized Bible programs frequently feature a built-in editor (some programs refer to this as the notepad) that allows the user to create, edit, and print out text documents. Various programs offer a wide range of word processing features, including inserting and deleting text, formatting text, centering, and pagination. The user can type personal notes, create outlines while studying the Bible, or jot down comments that pertain to a particular study, all while using other features of the program. The editor is often combined with the ability to cut and paste or transfer text from various Bible versions to the editor and related computerized resources. Bible verses and printouts from electronic sources (Strong's, Vine's, Bible encyclopedias, etc.) can be copied to this separate electronic work area for further study and use.

Verse Notes. Some programs include the ability to attach electronic notes directly to Bible verses. Unlike a notepad where the text is entered or transferred into a separate section of the program, in this feature the user is adding actual notes to words or verses in the electronic Bible text.

For example, you could call up John 3:16 and attach a note there, or alternately, you could call up the word *loved* and attach a note to that word. Then, later, you could retrieve either designation, and the note would still be there to read, edit, print, or delete.

Other Resources

Concordance. Concording is the basic function of all Bible study software. A concordance is a Bible index of all the words contained in the Bible with the references where each word may be found. It also designates by a unique number system what is the original Hebrew or Greek version of the word. The most widely used concordance, and one which is commonly available as a computer add-on, is Strong's *Concordance*, which is based exclusively on the King James Version.

Concordances are available for other versions of the Bible such as the New International Version (NIV), however, they are much less common than Strong's. Another widely used concordance is the Englishman's *Concordance*, which allows the user to find verses based on Strong's numbers rather than on the English word. Thus, instead of typing in *hell,* the user enters the Strong's number 1067, which represents *gĕĕnna,* the Greek word for hell.

Topical Bible. Similar to a concordance, this tool categorizes verses of the Bible by topic instead of by word. The most well-known topical Bible is *Nave's Topical Bible.* With a computerized Nave's, the user simply types in the selected topic, and the system searches for the topic and associated subtopics and provides a corresponding list of verses. The user can view the full text of these verses or can select a different Bible version and study the verses from that translation.

Greek and Hebrew Texts. Working with the Greek and Hebrew languages and Bible texts will be covered in detail in a separate chapter later in this book. These capabilities include working with Greek and Hebrew Bible texts, working with the transliterated languages, and doing searches on Greek and Hebrew words.

Bible Dictionaries and Encyclopedias. Bible dictionaries provide basic information on various Bible words, topics, customs, and traditions. The listings are arranged alphabetically and include background material such as historical, geographical, cultural, and archaeological information. The entries range from a sentence or

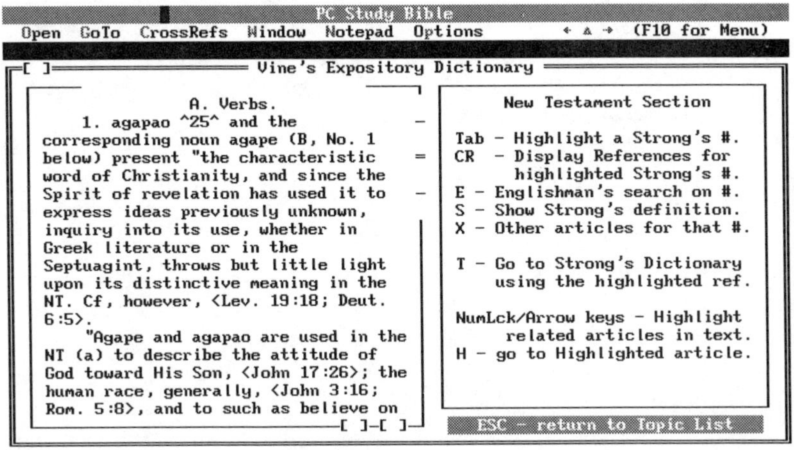

Fig. 3.2 Definition of *love* from *Vine's Expository Dictionary.* (Courtesy of Biblesoft.)

two to multipage articles. Bible dictionaries are a good starting point for research on people, places, and concepts. They provide not only a good overview of each subject, but, frequently, they refer to other books and resources for further research. The full text of many Bible dictionaries has been computerized and made available to users of Bible programs. Some are integrated into Bible study programs, while others are available through CD-ROM Bible libraries.

A Bible encyclopedia is an expanded Bible dictionary with longer articles that provide greater detail and information on more subjects. One advantage of a Bible encyclopedia is that it provides information on all different aspects of Bible background collected from various sources, such as the *Wycliffe Bible Encyclopedia* (Master Search Bible).

Dead Sea Scrolls

In 1947, a Bedouin shepherd who was looking for a lost goat came upon a cave located not far from Jericho and the Dead Sea in a region known as Qumran. Inside the cave (and the ten other caves that were found later) were approximately five hundred leather and papyrus scrolls of ancient Hebrew and Aramaic writings, stored in clay pots. These scrolls came to be known as the Dead Sea Scrolls.

The scrolls contained, among other things, a complete manuscript of the book of Isaiah, fragments of every Old Testament book except Esther, fourteen different manuscripts of Deuteronomy, ten manuscripts of Psalms, and other documents such as the Thanksgiving Psalms (similar to biblical Psalms), the War Scroll (plans for a battle between "sons of light" and "sons of darkness"), and the Genesis Apocryphon, a commentary on the Book of Genesis.

The significance of the Dead Sea Scrolls rests in the insights they give into the history of the Hebrew Scriptures. Prior to the discovery of these scrolls, the earliest known manuscripts dated back to the ninth century A.D. The Dead Sea Scrolls, however, dated back to the second century B.C. or earlier. The scrolls provided scholars with advanced understanding of certain biblical words as well as insight into the composition dates and origins of many of the books of the Old Testament. The scrolls also confirmed the existence of other texts aside from the Masoretic text.

The Dead Sea Scrolls, which were shown to a number of prominent scholars in 1947, were first thought by some to be forgeries.

However, manuscripts that were brought to the Hebrew University and the American School of Oriental Research were confirmed by scholars to be genuine and of tremendous value and significance. The Dead Sea Scrolls remain one of the most important discoveries in Old Testament manuscripts.

sources: Douglas, J. D., and Tenney, M. C., *New International Dictionary of the Bible* (Zondervan, 1987); Harrison, R. K. ed., *New Unger's Bible Dictionary* (Moody, 1988); Lockyer, H. ed., *Illustrated Bible Dictionary* (Nelson, 1986).

Bible Atlases. An understanding of Bible geography will greatly expand your understanding of the Bible. Bible atlases show not only the current political boundaries, but also indicate boundaries that existed in ancient Bible days. Some atlases include maps of events in biblical history, such as the journey of the Israelites in the Sinai Desert, the travels of Jesus, the missionary trips of Paul, and the locations of the various New Testament churches.

There are a number of computerized Bible atlases available, usually offered as add-on packages to a basic Bible software program. Not only do these products display full color maps on the screen, they also allow the user to print out copies for use in reports and biblical studies. The products include PC Bible Atlas by Parson's Technology and the maps offered by Bible Research Systems as a part of the The Word Processor program. There are also maps that are offered by CD-ROM based products such as on the CD Word Library and The New Bible Library.

Bible Commentaries. A commentary is a scholarly collection of analyses and interpretations of Bible texts. Commentaries provide a wealth of information about individual words, background, grammar, and syntax to explain and interpret the meaning of biblical texts. In addition to comments on each verse of the Bible, these tools also provide outlines, charts, and maps.

Miscellaneous Resources. Other computerized resources include books about manners and customs in Bible times, the historical geography of Bible lands, and biblical archaeology. (A full list of all these computer resources is provided in the reference section at the end of this book.)

Topical Indexes. The topical index feature that is included in some programs allows the user to create a list of verses that relate to a specified topic. This is particularly helpful because a word search, limited to a specific word or words, will not always identify all the verses where a certain topic or theme is discussed or addressed. Some programs offer precompiled indexes while others merely provide the capability to create the index.

User Interfaces

While user interface is not a feature in the same way that a search term or notepad is, it is a basic consideration in choosing a program that will actually be used rather than left on the shelf to collect dust.

User interface is a term for what a user sees when he or she interacts with a computer program. The design of an interface refers to the type and arrangement of the program's screens. For years most interfaces were completely text oriented; they simply provided pages and pages of textual information. Recently, however, the emphasis has been on interfaces that feature multiple "windows" and make extensive use of graphics. Commonly referred to as a GUI (graphical user interface) and pronounced "goo-ey," the most widely used graphics user interfaces are those on the Apple Macintosh and Microsoft Windows.

Currently, there are Bible programs written for DOS as well as for Microsoft Windows. Windows programs use the graphical Windows interface, while DOS programs vary widely in terms of available interfaces. Many DOS-based programs have their own built-in graphic user interface and support the use of multiple windows.

Mouse Support

Many Bible programs now allow the user to give commands with an electronic mouse in lieu of the standard keyboard. In program descriptions, this is commonly referred to as "mouse support." With the mouse the user can move a pointer around on the screen to the position of a desired command or icon (representing the command). When the mouse is clicked the command is executed. With windowed programs the user can move (drag) a window with NIV text from one part of the screen to another and can enlarge, shrink, or otherwise resize it at will. In short, the mouse simplifies the process of using a program.

Other Features

RAM Resident Feature. Some programs offer a feature that enables a user who is using a word processor program (external to the computerized Bible) to press a key sequence known as a "hot key" to bring the electronic Bible onto the screen in an instant. The program runs in memory so Bible verses from the computerized Bible can be sent (or "imported") to the word processor as though the user had typed in the verse. This option and how well it functions is based on the particular software and the amount of RAM memory that is available.

Text to Disk. Aside from printing text out directly or transferring information from the computerized Bible to a notepad or editor, some programs allow the user to save Bible text directly to a disk file, whether it be the verse that is on the screen or others that are specified.

Translations of the Bible

Individuals who work with computer Bible programs will be confronted with a range of translations to choose from. The following list discusses some of the characteristics and background of various Bible translations. While this information is by no means comprehensive or exhaustive, it can provide some insight into how the translations originated and how they differ.

American Standard Version (ASV). The ASV is the product of a revision of the King James Version, first published in 1901. The purpose of this revision was to account for problems resulting from outdated English and to integrate changes based on new knowledge gained from studies of the original Greek and Hebrew texts. While the ASV is considered a solid work of Bible scholarship, it has not been widely used because it gave little attention to the rhythm and style of the resulting translation.

Amplified Bible. This version, developed by editors at the Lockman Foundation, includes notes and text on translations, and footnotes concerning the text of the Bible.

Good News Bible. Written in plain and simple language, this version is designed to provide a fresh, new rendition of the Bible that is faithful to the ancient texts. One of the goals in creating this version was to achieve "dynamic equivalence," whereby the translation would offer the same effect as the original texts. This is especially good for young people and others who want more of a narrative account of the Bible. Sponsored by the American Bible Society, it is also known as Today's English Version; it was first published in 1976.

Jerusalem Bible. A version of the Bible produced by Roman Catholic scholars, it was published between 1956 and 1966. The text is based on a French Bible translated by the Dominican School in Jerusalem and was put into better English. This Bible is written in the Roman Catholic tradition.

King James Version (KJV). One of the oldest translations available (1611), this version bears the name of the man who authorized it, King James I of England. After ascending the throne, King James called a conference of bishops and clergy to discuss issues in the church. During that conference it was suggested that a new translation of the Bible should be created to replace the unpopular Bishop's Bible.

Fifty-four Greek and Hebrew scholars were selected for the task in 1604, but ultimately only forty-seven scholars worked on the translation. When work began in 1607, the scholars were divided into six groups: three for the Old Testament, two for the New Testament, and one for the Apocrypha (fifteen books that are not a part of the Hebrew Scripture texts, but were included in early Old Testament Bible editions). The groups met at Westminster, Cambridge, and Oxford, and rules were laid down on how the work would be conducted. The work was later reviewed by representatives from each panel, and differences were resolved in further meetings and in consultation with outside experts.

The scholars worked initially for two years (without any pay) and then spent nine more months in further revisions. The result, also known as the Authorized Version, has remained a popular and widely-used version for over three hundred years. Many additional study resources, such as the Strong's *Concordance*, were created to coordinate with the KJV.

Latin Vulgate Bible. This translation of the Old Testament into Latin was done by Jerome, who worked in a cave adjacent to the Grotto of the Nativity near Bethlehem. He translated the original Hebrew text into Latin and also referenced the Septuagint. Pope Damasus commissioned the work in A.D. 382, and it was completed in A.D. 405. The Vulgate Bible formed the basis for the Douay Bible, which is used by Roman Catholics.

Living Bible. This is the work of Kenneth N. Taylor, who paraphrased the Bible into simple English. Taylor started by paraphrasing the Apostle Paul's letters for his own children, then continued to paraphrase the rest of the Bible. Although not a true translation of the Bible, it has nevertheless been popular, especially among young people.

New American Bible. A Roman Catholic version of the Bible, first published in 1970.

New American Standard Bible (NASB). A revision of the American Standard Version (1901), this version was developed by the Lockman Foundation. Translated by a committee of conservative scholars, it is considered by some to have a style of English that is rougher than in other versions, however, it is favored by those who prefer a translation without extensive paraphrasing.

New Century Version (NCV). The New Century Version is a modern translation of the Scriptures. First published in 1987, it is designed to be faithful to the original Greek and Hebrew texts but written in a clear and easy-to-understand language. Word choice was based on the level used in the *World Book Encyclopedia,* and concepts are expressed in easily understandable terms. For instance, measurements are converted to modern equivalents, and modern names are used for some of the geographical locations. Ancient customs, rhetorical questions, figures of speech, obscure terms, and gender language are either explained or written clearly.

New King James Version (NKJV). This is an updated and revised version of the King James Version. The purpose of the revision was to preserve the KJV tradition, while making the words and grammar of the Bible more easily understandable and readable by a modern audience. Other goals of the translation were to preserve the majesty and rhythm of the original and to keep familiar passages as close to the original as possible.

New International Version (NIV). This modern translation of the Bible was created throughout a decade by a nondenominational team of more than one hundred scholars. It features a combination of modern-day, contemporary language and scholarly elements, including the texture and flow of more traditional translations.

New Revised Standard Version (NRSV). This updated version of the RSV takes into account recent archaeological findings such as the Dead Sea Scrolls.

Reina-Valera Actualizada (Spanish). This is a Spanish translation of the Bible.

Revised Standard Version (RSV). The RSV, another revision of the ASV of 1901, was prepared by a group of American scholars commissioned by the National Council of Churches. This revision, which maintained much of the quality of the KJV, includes the results of the latest Bible scholarship. This was first published in 1952.

In Closing

By now, you should have a good idea of what Bible software is all about. The features and functions that Bible programs offer encompass the entire range of Bible study from introductory to advanced. Aside from a comprehensive range of features including multiple versions, windowing, and associated resources, the benefits of speed, efficiency, and sophistication are evident. All of these can bring about significant improvements in how we study the Bible, which even in this high-tech computer age, by in large, is still being done manually just as it has been done for decades. However, with a computer, Bible software, and a willingness to learn an entirely new approach to studying God's word, you can be among the first to blaze a new frontier in Bible studies. And with all the time you save, you will have more time to study more of the Bible!

PART II

Examining Bible Computing Resources

Chapter Four

Parsing with Programs:
Greek and Hebrew Language Resources

> *"Hold fast the pattern of sound words
> which you have heard from me."*
> 2 Timothy 1:13 (NKJV)

I t's Greek to me!" is the standard complaint when people first encounter the original Bible languages—whether it be Aramaic, Hebrew, or Greek. The unfamiliar alphabets, unusual grammatical structures, and "foreign" appearance of these languages can discourage the person who wants to discover the riches of the ancient languages of the Bible. The suggestion that these languages could actually be used as a resource in Bible study seems a far-fetched proposal.

Yet while the casual student of the Bible might be able to avoid interacting with the original languages, anyone who is serious about doing comprehensive Bible studies should have at least a basic working knowledge of Greek and Hebrew, because a key to correctly interpreting the meaning of Scripture is to understand the meaning of Bible words in their original language.

Greek and Hebrew Resources

Whether you want to study the words of the Bible, or learn Hebrew and Greek, or complete advanced grammatical analyses, there are computer resources available to help you. In fact, there are programs and resources that allow the user to work successfully with the original Greek and Hebrew without any previous knowledge of these languages. There are also programs designed for learning Greek and Hebrew, and some for working with the original language texts. For more advanced studies, there are programs for parsing, as well as lexical and grammatical searches of biblical words. Now, let's examine these resources in more detail.

Greek and Hebrew Study Aids

Some people are put off by a suggestion to study the meaning of Greek and Hebrew words because they think that only those who have studied these languages at length can be successful in this endeavor. However, with the many Bible study tools and resources available today, the lack of specialized training in Greek or Hebrew is not a hindrance to a thorough study of original Bible words and phrases.

English translations are useful as a starting point for Bible studies, but a deeper level of comprehension is gained by studying the different nuances and shades of meaning that are found only in the original Greek and Hebrew—which, in general, are more precise than English. That is why approximately 11,280 different words from the original languages were used in the Bible, but only 6,000 English words were used in the translation.

How did this happen? Basically, because several words in the original language were translated by one English word. For example, the word *love* was used to translate both Greek words *agapaō* (ἀγαπάω) and *philéō* (φιλέω). And the word *other* was used to translate seven Greek words, including *állos* (ἄλλος), *heteros* (ἕτερος), *loipos* (λοιπος), *allótriŏs* (ἀλλότριος), *allēlōn* (ἀλλήλων), *heis* (εἰς), and *ĕkĕinŏs* (ἐκεῖνος). Since each of these Greek words conveys a meaning that is distinct from the others, it is clear that the one English word cannot capture the various nuances of meaning conveyed by this variation. That is why we gain the most accurate understanding of the Bible by considering the original language words and tracing how those words are used in different Bible contexts.

As a further complexity, in some cases, a single Greek word is translated by an entire phrase in English. Consider this verse in 2 Corinthians 3:18: "But we all, with open face beholding as in a glass the glory of the Lord, are changed into the same image from glory to glory, even as by the Spirit of the Lord" (KJV). The Greek word *katŏptrizŏmai* (κατοπτρίζομαι) was translated into the English phrase "beholding as in a glass." In other instances, a Greek word was translated into one or more different words in English. For example, in the KJV the Greek word *kŏinōnia* (κοινωνία) is translated as *fellowship, communion, communication, contribution,* and *distribution.*

The original Greek and Hebrew words are invaluable sources of insight into the precise meaning of biblical texts. Fortunately, the student of the Bible today has many electronic resources available to help in researching and analyzing these words. There are programs that aid in doing word studies; programs that search for the original language equivalent of an English word, verse, or passage; and programs that provide computerized resources such as concordances, word dictionaries, lexicons, and Bible dictionaries. In the following pages we will discuss some of these resources and how they can help in original Bible language study.

Concordances

One of the basic tools for finding the meaning of a Hebrew or Greek word is the concordance. While numerous concordances have been available in print form for many years, only recently have some of these been made available in an electronic form for use with the computer.

Strong's *Concordance* (KJV). This resource lists all the verses that contain a certain English word, and each use of the word is keyed to its corresponding word in Greek or Hebrew. Each Greek and Hebrew word that is used in the Bible and its definition is tagged with an identification number (Strong's number). This number can also be used to reference the same word in other works such as *New Englishman's Greek Concordance* and *Vine's Expository Dictionary of Old and New Testament Words.* This concordance is available on a wide variety of electronic Bible packages.

New Englishman's Hebrew/Aramaic Concordance. This concordance locates verses based on the original Hebrew words instead of on the English word as in Strong's. However, words can also be identified with Strong's numbers. One program that features a computerized version of this concordance is Biblesoft's PC Study Bible.

New Englishman's Greek Concordance. Based on the same concept as the Hebrew/Aramaic version, this concordance is also available on Biblesoft's PC Study Bible.

Lexicons and Dictionaries

Greek-English Lexicon of the New Testament by W. Bauer, W. F. Arndt, F. W. Gingrich, and F. W. Danker, provides an authoritative and detailed definition of every Greek word in the Bible. It requires a knowledge of the Greek alphabet and is available on CD Word Library (CD-ROM).

Vine's Expository Dictionary of Old and New Testament Words by W. E. Vine, M. F. Unger, and W. White, Jr., provides the definition, origin, and usage of each Greek and Hebrew word in the Bible. However, it does not require a knowledge of Greek or Hebrew because the words are organized according to English usage. It is available on Biblesoft PC Study Bible (add-on) and The New Bible Library (CD-ROM).

Intermediate and Advanced Resources

Theological Wordbook of the Old Testament, volumes 1 and 2, edited by R. L. Harris, G. L. Archer, and B. K. Waltke, is a comprehensive reference source to the Hebrew words in the Old Testament, with a focus on the theological meanings of each word. Words are keyed to the Strong's numbering system. It is available on The New Bible Library (CD-ROM).

An exhaustive reference source, the *Theological Dictionary of the New Testament,* edited by G. Kittel and G. Friedrich (its single volume, abridged version is commonly known as "little Kittel"), lists over 2,300 significant New Testament words. It discusses how they are used in the Bible, what is the secular Greek background of each, and how each relates to the Old Testament and other ancient literature. This resource is available through the CD Word Library, on CD-ROM.

Greek Language-Learning Tools

If you want to learn biblical Greek, the computer can be your tutor. Several programs have been developed that provide presentations of Greek vocabulary and grammar and tools such as flashcard drills to help in learning this language.

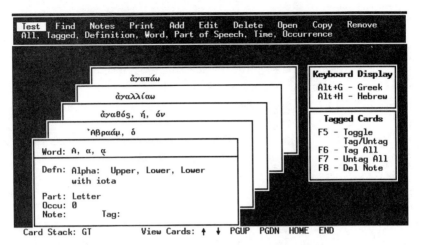

Fig. 4.1 Greek word flashcards. (Courtesy of Parsons Technology.)

GREEK TOOLS. Published by Parson's Technology, this complete program, including software and text, has a wide range of features that will help both the beginning and the advanced student to learn and work effectively with biblical Greek. The complete package includes the program, a reference manual, and a copy of John Dobson's book, *Learn New Testament Greek* (Baker).

There are five main parts to the program: a Greek Lexicon Database, a Grammar Guide and Reference, a Manuscript Evidences Database, a section on textual criticism, and a Greek-Hebrew-English word processor. The first two are designed mainly for beginning students in Greek while the last three are geared towards advanced students and Greek scholars.

The Greek lexicon database features an innovative flash card system of drills for learning Greek vocabulary. Drills can be designed according to personal preference, and the system will record performance. There are actually two databases of Greek words in this system: the primary database holds approximately 1,180 cards, featuring words that occur 10 or more times in the Greek New Testament, and the secondary database includes 48 additional stacks of flash cards incorporating the words presented in the *Learn New Testament Greek* text.

The Greek Grammar Guide is an electronic reference text. In essence, it captures about two years of college-level Greek in summary form and discusses such topics as the alphabet, parts of speech (including nouns, pronouns, verbs, and all others), rules for breathing and accents, and information on diphthongs and punctuation.

The manuscript catalog allows the user to analyze various Greek New Testament manuscripts, each represented on a separate card. The program also offers a worksheet to evaluate the results from each text analysis.

The textual criticism section of the program provides information about sources of Bible manuscripts, with discussions about how they have been classified and what criterion was used to make these classifications. The program also offers the ability to edit the textual criticism file.

Finally, the program offers an editor that allows word processing in English, Greek, and Hebrew. Aside from creating and editing text, the user can print out files, create ASCII (text-only) data files, and import (receive and integrate) text files from other word processors.

The program not only provides an organized approach to learning the Greek language but also provides supplementary materials that enable the user to become knowledgeable about Greek texts and manuscripts.

MEMCARDS GREEK VOCABULARY. This program is designed to help the user learn Greek words through drills and other memorization techniques. The program features large, readable characters, as well as a high-speed drill method that moves the learning process along at a fast pace.

The system monitors performance and calculates short- and long-term retention for each word. From there, the program will categorize the word cards into groups based on short-term memorization, long-term memorization, or no memorization at all.

With this program the user can create new word cards, edit existing ones, do sequential drilling of a stack of cards, or even print out study sheets of the cards for personal reference. There are more than 1,400 words contained in the program including those that appear ten times or more in the Greek New Testament.

MEMCARDS GREEK FORMS AND PARSING. Using the same approach as the GREEK VOCABULARY, this program tests for knowledge of Greek grammar. It features hundreds of grammar tables and forms, which are presented in a drill format, and includes verb conjugations, parsing, noun declensions, and a review of other grammatical forms. In total, over 2,400 Greek forms are represented in the data that was derived from the Gramcord Institute's grammatically tagged New Testament database.

The Greek Vocabulary and Greek Forms and Parsing are available as a packaged set known as the **GREEK STUDENT'S BUNDLE.**

Hebrew Language-Learning Tools

HEBREW TOOLS is a comprehensive program, published by Parson's Technology, that is designed to help the user learn biblical Hebrew. The package comes complete with a copy of the program, the user manual, and a copy of Manahem Mansoor's text, *Biblical Hebrew: Step By Step* (Baker).

There are three main components to the HEBREW TOOLS program: a Hebrew Tools Lexicon, a Hebrew Grammar Guide, and the Hebrew Tools Editor. Basically, the words in the lexicon are presented in a flashcard format (including the Hebrew word, its definition, and grammatical structure) that allows the user to test his or her knowledge of Hebrew. It is also possible to create personal cards, to edit cards, and to delete cards from a stack.

In addition, the program provides tools for studying Hebrew grammar, including summary tables and presentations of the Hebrew alphabet, parts of speech, strong and weak verbs, as well as rules for proper pronunciation. The Hebrew Grammar Guide is a summarization of approximately one year of seminary-level Hebrew.

Finally, the HEBREW TOOLS editor allows the user to actually work with Hebrew, as well as Greek and English. The editor displays Hebrew and Greek on the screen using the original alphabets.

HEBREW WORDMASTER I & II. This program uses drills, quizzes, and games to teach Hebrew vocabulary. Exercises, include Spell-It, Match-It, and Displays.

LEARNING TO READ HEBREW. Even those who have no previous knowledge of the Hebrew alphabet can learn to read with this program. Geared to Hebrew beginners, it also enforces the teaching with an audio tape. Reviews and quizzes test learning levels.

HEBREW TOOLS. This program (different from Parsons Technology software of the same name) is uniquely designed to increase proficiency in Hebrew. A Vocabulary Builder module improves the general knowledge of Hebrew words, and the Hebrew text editor allows the user to create and save text files in Hebrew.

MEMCARDS BIBLICAL HEBREW VOCABULARY. Produced by Memorization Technology, this program uses the same high-speed drill method as the GREEK VOCABULARY program. It provides basic language learning drills and measures user retention of word items. Over 1,400 words are included in the program; the first 1,000 are categorized by frequency in the Old Testament—inclusion required that a word be used at least 29 times. The program is keyed to several textbooks on Hebrew.

HAMMOREH. This Hebrew grammar tutorial program teaches the complexities of Hebrew grammar using a unique approach of onscreen color and movement. With VGA color graphics, the self-paced program is broken down into a series of lessons including Introduction to the Hebrew Alphabet, Grammatical Forms in Biblical Hebrew, and lessons on the strong and weak verbs.

Original Greek and Hebrew Texts

The original Greek and Hebrew Bible texts are much more accessible than you might think! Many of the Bible software packages on the market feature not only English translations such as the KJV or NIV, but also the original Greek and Hebrew texts. Well-known titles of the original texts such as the *Biblica Hebraica Stuttgartensia*, the Nestle-Aland United Bible Society *Greek New Testament*, and *Textus Receptus*, are available in an electronic format for reading, searching, and analytical study.

Currently, Greek and Hebrew texts are available as parts of disk-based programs, as well as in CD-ROM Bible libraries. In many cases, the original language texts do not come with the base package of a program but must be acquired separately as optional add-on modules. Since Greek and Hebrew Bible texts usually do not include an English translation, a basic knowledge of Greek or Hebrew is generally required to work effectively with these tools.

But what can you do with these ancient language texts? To begin with, if you have knowledge of Greek and/or Hebrew, you can translate the texts yourself either for an exegesis or other advanced studies. Also, depending on the software you are using, you can set up a Greek or Hebrew text in a separate screen window much like any other Bible version and then set up parallel English translations for comparison. An English and a Greek text, for example, can be linked together to display the same verses at the same time. Some programs that allow verse notes in the English versions also allow notes to be attached to verses in the Greek and Hebrew texts.

An added advantage is that many of the Greek and Hebrew texts available with commercial software packages are tagged, that is description codes about the grammatical form of the word, its root, and other information are attached to individual words. With these tags the user can do complex word searches and gather pertinent information on word meanings.

Greek New Testament. The original text of the New Testament usually consists of the Greek text with little, if any, computerized explanatory material; however, texts are usually tagged to allow for searches and other computer operations. The text is frequently broken down into chapters and verses.

There are a number of different Greek New Testament texts available including the Nestle-Aland 26th edition of the *Novum Testamentum Graece*, the United Bible Society (UBS) 3rd Edition *Greek New Testament, Byzantine/Majority Textform*, and the *Textus Receptus* (Stephen's 1550 and Scrivener's 1891).

Silver Mountain's LBASE and Bible Windows, Logos Bible Software, Hermenutika's BibleWord Plus and BibleWorks for Windows, the Word Advanced Study System, Zondervan's BibleSource, and the CDWord Library offer Greek New Testament texts with their programs.

Hebrew Old Testament. The original Hebrew text of the Old Testament is also available, and one of the most widely used versions is the *Biblica Hebraica Stuttgartensia* (BHS).

The Word Advanced Study System, Silver Mountain's Bible Windows and LBASE, Logos Bible Software, Hermenutika's Bible Word Plus and Bible Works for Windows, and other programs offer Hebrew Old Testament texts.

Septuagint (LXX) Greek Old Testament. A Greek translation of the Hebrew Old Testament, the Septuagint is also available through various vendors such as Hermenutika's Bible Works for Windows and BibleWord Plus, Silver Mountain's Bible Windows and LBASE, and Logos Bible Software.

CD Word Library provides many tools for working with the Greek texts including the Nestle-Aland *Greek New Testament*, as well as Rahlf's Septuagint, which is linked to the English Bible translations. The program also features three Greek lexicon resources, including the *Bauer Greek-English Lexicon of the New Testament*, the *Intermediate Greek-English Lexicon* by Liddell and Scott, and the *Theological Dictionary of the New Testament*, edited by Kittel and Friedrich.

The Septuagint

The Septuagint, a translation of the Old Testament from Hebrew into Greek, holds a unique place in history as one of the first major translations of a library of books. It allowed the Greek-speaking peoples of the time to benefit from the riches and truths of the Hebrew Scriptures.

Sometimes referred to as the LXX (meaning seventy), the Septuagint was created during the second and third centuries ʙ.ᴄ. The Pentateuch (Genesis, Exodus, Leviticus, Numbers, Deuteronomy) was translated during the reign of Ptolemy Philadelphus (285–246 ʙ.ᴄ.). The use of the LXX designation was believed to be an approximation of the seventy-two translators, six from each of the twelve tribes of Israel. It could also have referred to the seventy elders of Israel mentioned in Exodus 24:1 and 9.

The Septuagint was widely used by the Alexandrian Jews and became the Bible of early Christianity before the New Testament was written. It opened up the truths of creation, sin, and redemption to a much wider population than could be reached through the original Hebrew texts. In fact, Jesus and the New Testament writers quoted frequently both from the Septuagint as well as from the Hebrew Scriptures.

There have been countless manuscripts and revisions of the Septuagint under such names as the *Codex Vaticanus, Codex Sinaiticus,* and the *Codex Ephraemi Rescriptus.*

Sources: Douglas, J. D. and Tenney, M. C., *New International Dictionary of the Bible* (Zondervan, 1987); Harrison, R. K. ed., *New Unger's Bible Dictionary* (Moody, 1988); Lockyer, H. ed., *Illustrated Bible Dictionary* (Nelson, 1986).

Advanced Tools for Greek/Hebrew Studies

Advanced students of the Bible may want to study the words of the Bible from the perspective of the original languages rather than from English. Such studies might include doing single word searches in Greek and Hebrew to find all the verses that have a specified form of the word and multiple-word searches to find verses that contain more than one Greek (or Hebrew) word. (Multiple-word searches in Greek and Hebrew can also be done using Boolean operators such as AND, OR, XOR, and NOT.)

Another type of search in the original languages is known as a lexical search. This search locates verses that contain all the words based on a specified lexical root. Aside from word searches and lexical searches, some programs also allow phrase searches, based either on a specified Greek or Hebrew phrase or on the lexical roots of a phrase. Finally, a valuable search for advanced students is the grammatical search. This tool allows the user to specify a search based on a word's form of speech (including noun, adjective, adverb, preposition, conjunction, and many others), on tense, voice, mood, and person.

As an additional feature, some programs provide parsing information for each of the words in the original texts. By opening a window and typing in a few keystrokes, the user can receive complete parsing information on any word in the original Greek and Hebrew texts.

The availability of these features in a program depends on whether it is designed to be a general-purpose "Bible text and concordance" tool or a more advanced Greek and Hebrew study resource. Some programs offer these advanced tools as an integrated part of the entire package; in other instances the program is an individual package designed specifically for working with the Greek and Hebrew languages and texts.

In the following paragraphs, we will briefly discuss each of the programs that offer specialized Greek and Hebrew analysis tools and will emphasize the special features they provide.

BIBLE WINDOWS. While many Bible software programs emphasize various English translations, this program features the Greek and Hebrew texts that are provided in Microsoft Windows. The versions supported by the program include the KJV, the RSV, tagged Greek New Testament, tagged Greek Old Testament, Latin Vulgate, and tagged Septuagint.

One innovative aspect of this program is its optional interlinear display. This means that if you are studying in the Greek New

Testament, and you choose the interlinear display, the system will display the original Greek text, an analysis of the text, and the dictionary form of the word.

Other features include parsing, searches, and multiple windows (the user can view the Greek New Testament, an English translation, the Hebrew Old Testament, and additional details on Greek words all on the same screen).

BIBLE WORD PLUS. This DOS-based program allows the user to study the original texts, including the Greek New Testament (UBS 3rd edition/Nestle Aland 26th), BHS Hebrew Old Testament, and Rahlf's LXX Septuagint. The program features pointed and cantillated Hebrew, fully accented Greek, and the ability to do complex searches (roots, prefixes, suffixes, or precise phrases) in both Greek and Hebrew. The user can set between three to twelve synchronized and scrolled windows to display English, Greek, and Hebrew simultaneously on the same screen.

BIBLE WORKS FOR WINDOWS. This Microsoft Windows program offers a wide range of features from intermediate to advanced levels of Bible study. It offers the KJV, the RSV, and the ASV, all keyed and indexed to Strong's and Englishman's numbers. In terms of lexicons, it provides the *Greek-English Lexicon of the New Testament* (abridged) by J. H. Thayer, with 5,624 definitions that are keyed to Strong's numbers (and pages in the *Theological Dictionary of the New Testament*), as well as *A Hebrew and English Lexicon of the Old Testament* (abridged) by F. Brown, S. Driver, and C. Briggs, with 8,674 definitions keyed to Strong's numbers and referenced to Harris's *Theological Wordbook of the Old Testament.*

The Hebrew Old Testament and both Greek Testaments are lexically and grammatically analyzed. The Hebrew text uses Westminster Theological Seminary's WTS Searchable Morphological Analysis with complete parsings and lexical forms, while the Greek text features the UBS *Greek-English Dictionary of the New Testament* by Barclay M. Newman, Jr. and the CCAT-UBS 3rd Greek New Testament with Complete Searchable Morphology/ Parsings and lexical forms. Strong's and Englishman's numbers, lexicons, and parsing/morphology tools can also be used with these texts.

The parsing information provided by the program's module displays verb information including stem, aspect, person, gender, number, and state. Other parts of speech, including nouns, pronouns, adjectives, and participles are completely analyzed as well.

GRAMCORD. The Gramcord program is a Greek word concordance system that is extremely helpful in doing detailed syntactical and lexical studies in the Greek New Testament. The program allows for both grammatical and lexical searches, and together with the GRAMBUILD program, can create searches using a menu-driven interface with extensive online help. The GRAMPLOT module provides graphical plots of various New Testament Greek statistics, as well as stylistic and linguistic maps.

One facet of the GRAMCORD program is GRAMSEARCH. The strength of this tool is its rapid search capabilities through the Greek New Testament. Not only does it provide all the New Testament occurrences, but it lists all the different forms of a particular Greek word as well. Another facet of GRAMCORD is GRAMGREEK, which converts scriptural references into their full Greek New Testament verse forms. It allows the user to convert a reference, whether Revelation 22:21 or John chapters 1–3, into its full text form (Nestle-Aland 26th Edition Greek New Testament) in the multilingual word processor.

LBASE is an advanced study tool that allows the user to effectively analyze and study Greek, Hebrew, and Latin Bible texts. The program provides for searches based on grammatical constructions, as well as on words and phrases. In addition, the user can design a "custom concordance" according to specific grammatical search criteria. LBASE works with multiple windows so various Bible versions can be displayed on the screen simultaneously and linked together. English translations are available as well as the Greek New Testament and the Hebrew Old Testament.

LOGOS BIBLE SOFTWARE provides a number of features for studying the original Bible texts and languages. The program integrates well with Microsoft Windows with the use of multiple on-screen windows, menu bars, and icons.

For studies using concordances and lexicons, LOGOS BIBLE SOFTWARE allows easy access to Strong's numbers, an enhanced form of Strong's Greek and Hebrew dictionary, and cross-references to the *Treasury of Scripture Knowledge*.

Logos Research also offers a wide selection of original Greek and Hebrew texts including the Nestle-Aland/UBS 3rd edition, the Byzantine/Majority Textform, the Textus Receptus (Stephen's 1550), and the Biblica Hebraica Stuttgartensia.

For more advanced studies, they offer the Tense, Voice, Mood module (TVM). This program allows the user to instantly search the King James Version according to the tense, voice, and mood for any Greek or Hebrew verb. It is programmed in conjunction with Strong's *Concordance* to provide detailed information on Greek and Hebrew verbs and verb forms.

PARSER PLUS. With PARSER PLUS, the user simply types in a Scripture reference and the program provides a complete grammatical breakdown of the Greek text for that reference. The amount of parsing and the boundaries of the parsing are designated by the user.

THE WORD ADVANCED STUDY SYSTEM. This Wordsoft program offers the Greek New Testament (UBS 3rd edition), the Hebrew Old Testament (Westminster Hebrew Morphological Database), along with the KJV, NKJV AND NRSV English Bibles and the

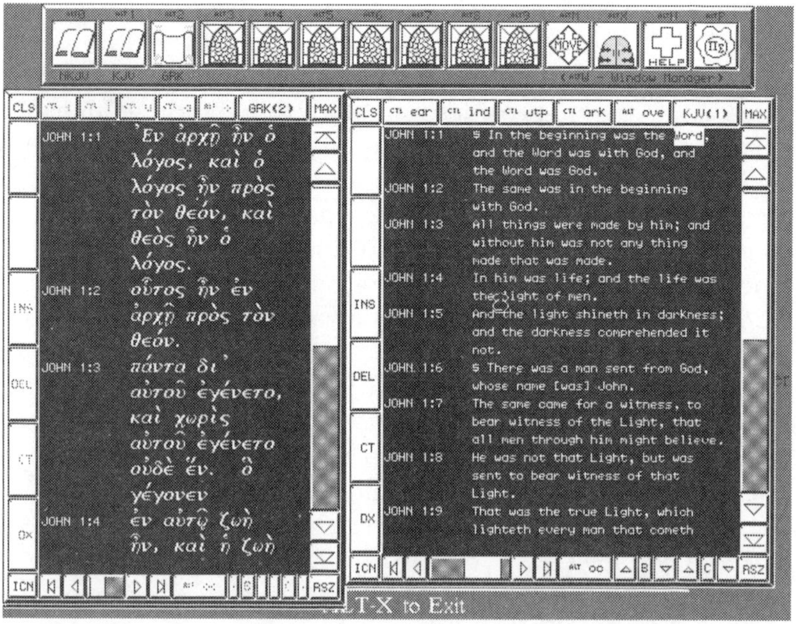

Fig. 4.2 Comparative study of Greek and English passages. (Courtesy of Word, Inc.)

Strong's dictionary-concordance. A unique feature provided to the user is the inclusion of the Bible Text Converter software that enables the user to process Bible versions from other software packages. Complete lexical and grammatical searching is made simple by point and click menus. Parsing of all Greek and Hebrew words can be instantly displayed with one key stroke.

This program offers one of the widest ranges of search features available. The TRANSFER feature simplifies searching for words or phrases by allowing the user to paste any displayed word or phrase from the verse display into the search window. There is also a FIND feature that allows the user to type in part of the word (in transliterated form) and then choose the correct word from an exhaustive word list.

Searches can be performed in up to ten independent or sychronized windows with multiple Bible versions for an interlinear effect. Greek and Hebrew appear on the screen in their original character forms. The integrated English-Greek-Hebrew-European-Yiddish text editor allws cut and paste of Bible texts into a document that can be printed on any nearly printer. Also, this editor allows personal notes to be attached anywhere within a text. Hebrew can be entered in a true right-to-left mode with correct word wrapping. Underlining, linedrawing, and text critical symbols are also available.

The easy to use windowing environment allows resizeable and moveable windows. When the user closes a study session, all of his windows' contents are saved and then restored the next time the program is loaded.

In Closing

The capabilities of Bible software go far beyond English translations. Because advanced students and scholars of the Bible want and need to study the Greek and Hebrew languages, to analyze original language texts, and also to scrutinize the original words of the Bible in considerable detail, a wide range of computerized Bible resources have been developed to meet these needs. Electronic tools are available for language learning, for grammatical analysis, and for investigation of the actual Greek and Hebrew texts. These are invaluable Bible study tools; not only do they save considerable time by automating complex, tedious tasks, but they accomplish these tasks efficiently and correctly.

Chapter Five

The Tower of Babel on a Disk:
Using Multilingual Word Processors

"The place is called Babel since that is where the LORD confused the language of the whole world."
Genesis 11:9 (NCV)

H ave you ever wanted to work on the computer with a language other than English? Perhaps you wanted to display the Hebrew or Greek language in its original form when you prepared sermon notes, or a paper, an article or a manuscript.

While conventional word processors work with the English language and sometimes offer the capability to reproduce selected foreign language characters, they are less useful if an individual wants to work with foreign languages such as Greek and Hebrew. However, there is a class of programs that makes it possible to work directly with a wide variety of languages. These programs are known as multilingual word processors. They provide powerful capabilities for working with foreign languages, even with those that have unusual alphabets. The Bible student will find these programs particularly helpful for composing work in Greek or Hebrew and for printing the work out in the original language form.

This chapter will serve as a general introduction to multilingual word processors. We will discuss what they are, what they can do, what major products are on the market, and how to determine whether you need to use one. Since a multilingual word processor is not something that every student of the Bible needs to have, we encourage readers to determine the validity of their need based on the advantages and disadvantages that are presented here. However, there is no question that those who work regularly with Greek, Hebrew, or other languages will not want to be without the indispensable help of one of these programs.

What Is a Multilingual Word Processor?

In many ways a multilingual word processor is similar to the word processors we use every day—they allow us to enter, save, edit, and print out text. However, the main difference between a multilingual program such as MULTILINGUAL SCHOLAR and a standard word processor such as WordPerfect is that the multilingual program allows the user to work with foreign alphabets and words, often as easily as working with English.

Advantages

What are some of the features and benefits of multilingual word processors?

1. **They work with a variety of language characters**. The basic reason for working with a multilingual word processor is to write in a specific foreign language. (For Bible study purposes this would be either Greek or Hebrew.) In fact, with a multilingual processor it is possible to work with many languages. For instance, MULTILINGUAL SCHOLAR comes complete with five different alphabets: Arabic, Cyrillic (Russian), Greek, Hebrew, and English. Those who want to work with more exotic languages, such as Chinese, Indian, or Mongolian, can simply purchase these languages and fonts as add-on packages.

2. **They provide easy entry of foreign language characters.** Multilingual word processors are designed to help you write easily in foreign languages. The programs provide a simple process for creating complicated alphabets and displaying them to the

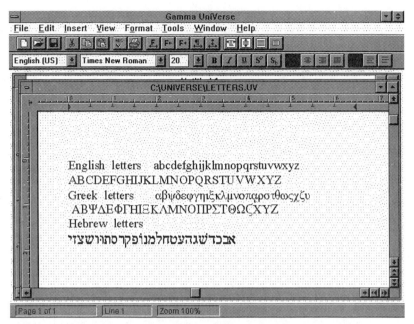

Fig. 5.1 Multiple language fonts in a multilingual word processor. (Courtesy of Gamma Prod.)

screen as fully formed characters. With a multilingual word processor you are not limited to the transliterated forms of Greek and Hebrew, instead, you can type in the actual language characters and see them on the screen. In computer terms, it is a form of WYSIWYG (What You See Is What You Get), both on the screen and on paper.

3. **They print out documents in the foreign language**. Many multilingual word processors include fonts (typefaces) that furnish exact reproductions of Greek and Hebrew (and other language) letters. In fact, for some languages, programs offer more than one style of typeface.

4. **They allow easy integration of English with foreign languages.** With most multilingual word processors, you can work in English as well as in foreign languages. This is an important capability especially if you are creating an article, book, or paper on the Bible that is primarily written in English, yet you want to include words, verses, and quotations in Greek or Hebrew. While this would be difficult to accomplish with a standard word processor, with a multilingual program it is easy.

Disadvantages

Before you run out to buy a multilingual word processor, however, you should assess the drawbacks as well.

1. **Usage may be limited.** A multilingual word processor is definitely not something that every student of the Bible needs to have. Those who seldom want to write in Greek or Hebrew will find that the expense and time required to work with one of these processors is just not worth the money and effort. On the other hand, those who work regularly with Greek, Hebrew, or one of several other languages, will find this type of processor an indispensable tool.

2. **It is necessary to learn a new program**. Any new program requires time to learn, and multilingual word processors are no exception. To use one successfully, it is necessary to become familiar not only with a variety of fonts but also with the special keys and key sequences that create the unique markings required for Greek and Hebrew words. In addition, it is necessary to learn how to use a standard computer keyboard to define each of the special characters, and it will take time to understand how the system creates text in different languages, many of which work quite differently from English.

Depending on the package, a multilingual word processor may either be similar or totally different from your existing word processor. In any case, you will probably need to learn a number of new keys and commands.

3. **The software is an added expense.** A multilingual word processor can easily cost hundreds of dollars and may require optional add-on packages for languages that are not part of the standard package.

4. **A laser or high resolution printer is strongly recommended.** While you can print out Greek and Hebrew on a dot-matrix printer, the slow printing and quality of the characters is inferior to what can be done with a laser printer. In fact, many of the fonts available work best with a laser printer.

5. **Working with a foreign language is complex**. Typing in English text is easy—you just type as though you were using a typewriter. However, typing in a language such as Hebrew is totally different in arrangement, form, and organization. In order to create a Hebrew sentence you have to be familiar with both Hebrew grammatical construction and with a Hebrew keyboard.

Features of Multilingual Word Processors

Basic Features

A multilingual word processor offers many of the basic features common to all word processors such as entering, saving, formatting, and editing text. With a multilingual word processor you can create a new file of text, make changes in it, save it, retrieve it to and from the disk, print it out, and also format the text in various ways.

In addition, most multilingual word processors include such basic text processing capabilities as searching for text and replacing it with something else, pagination, hyphenation, and displaying simple graphics.

Additional Word Processing Features

Many of the multilingual word processors presently on the market also include scientific and technical word processing capabilities. These are useful for creating papers, theses, and reports, in particular those of an academic or technical nature.

For instance, in addition to Greek and Hebrew word processing, products in this class provide the ability to create mathematical and scientific symbols, complex math and statistics equations, chemical structures, superscripts and subscripts, as well as footnotes and endnotes.

As in English language word processors, the multilingual word processors frequently provide a range of fonts (typefaces) to choose from as well as a variety of formatting methods, such as underlining, italics, and boldface.

The Written Greek Language

The Greek language appears somewhat familiar to many of us since Greek letters such as alpha (α), beta (β), sigma (σ), and chi (ξ) appear frequently in math formulas, in statistics, and even as names of college honor societies and student groups.

The Greek of the New Testament and the Septuagint (LXX) is known as Koine or Common Greek. This was the form of Greek that was spoken by the common people. It is different from classical Greek (as in Greek classical literature) and Modern Greek, which is used in Greece today.

Written Greek consists of two main parts: the words composed of Greek alphabets, and various accents and breathing marks. The Greek alphabet is as follows:

αβγδεζηθικλμνξοπρστυφχψω

ΑΒΓΔΕΖΗΘΙΚΛΜΝΞΟΠΡΣΤΥΦΧΨΩ

Greek text can also have accents and breathing marks, as follows:

᾿ ῾ ˘ ´ ` ῀ ¨ ᾳ

These combine to create Greek words, such as:

κύριος	kuriŏs	Lord
᾿αγαπάω	agapaō	God's love
φιλέω	philĕō	tender affection
λόγοσ	lŏgŏs	word
γέεννα	gĕĕnna	hell
ἅδης	hadēs	place of departed spirits

Greek and Hebrew Language Features

There are a number of multilingual word processors on the market, and many offer languages other than Greek and Hebrew. For example some offer the Cyrillic (Russian) alphabet, Arabic, Japanese, as well as a variety of other languages used around the world. However, since the focus in this book is on Bible study, we will emphasize the Greek and Hebrew language features of these programs.

Greek. The Greek language, which is the basis of the New Testament and the Greek translation of the Old Testament (Septuagint or LXX), is written using not only the Greek alphabet but also special symbols, including accents, breathing marks, and other diacritics.

Word processors that support Greek allow the user to transform an English keyboard into one that can produce Greek, including both the alphabet and special symbols. Typically, the Greek keyboard is activated by typing a unique set of keystrokes or function keys. To do this, many multilingual word processors use what is known as a mnemonic approach. This means that the Greek letters are "mapped" (made to correspond) to English letters through logical sight or sound relationships that are easy to remember.

For instance, the Greek letter alpha (a) would correspond to the "A" key, while the Greek beta (β) would be designated by the "B" key, gamma (γ) with the "G" key, and so on. The Greek letters are mapped to an approximate English equivalent.

Letters that do not relate obviously to an English letter are designated by phonetic (sound) correspondence to an English equivalent. For example, the English letter "F" would be used to type the character phi (ϕ) or "C" to type the Greek chi (χ).

The Greek text is not complete, however, without accents and breathing marks. These must be added after the letters have been typed, so creating a Greek document is a two-step process that is a bit more complex than English word processing. Yet, in general, writing Greek text is not difficult because the alphabet is generally familiar (it is used in other disciplines such as mathematics, statistics, and the humanities), and the shapes of Greek letters are not too far removed from that of English letters.

Frequently, multilingual word processors offer a variety of Greek fonts in different styles to suit the needs of a particular document or audience. In addition, some allow a choice between biblical (Koine), classical, and modern Greek.

Hebrew. The Hebrew language is perceived to be more difficult than Greek especially to those who are unfamiliar with the biblical languages. This is natural because the Hebrew alphabet is extremely different from the English and other Western alphabets, and the structure of the words is also vastly different.

Another basic difference is that the Hebrew language is read from right to left, the exact opposite of Western languages. In addition, the words are read from top to bottom, and each word can have up to three separate components: the consonant, which is the dominant symbol of the word; adjacent vowel points, which indicate the weight or accentuation given to the word; and, in some cases, cantellations, which originated in the Middle Ages to help cantors sing the text.

Multilingual word processors have been designed to help you create these complex words using a mnemonic approach similar in concept to that used for Greek words. Basically, when you select the Hebrew language, your keyboard is adapted to write in

Hebrew, complete with designated consonants and vowel points that are used to compose each word.

While the specific layout depends on the program, it is often possible to choose between different keyboard layouts and Hebrew fonts. Some keyboards are arranged in a mnemonic approach that is based on sounds, appearance of the symbols, or other memory aid techniques. Another type of keyboard is the Israeli Typewriter Layout, which corresponds to the Hebrew typewriter keyboard and the IBM Modern Hebrew DOS.

The mnemonic approach for the Hebrew alphabet maps consonants to the sound (and transliterated form) of the word: for example, the consonant bet (ב) is mapped to the English letter "B" and the consonant zayin (ז) to the English letter "Z". Sometimes, a Hebrew consonant is mapped to the particular word it resembles, such as alep (א) to the English "X" or tet (ט) to the letter "U".

Some programs provide both the biblical Hebrew and modern Hebrew fonts.

The Hebrew Language

The Hebrew language comes from the Phoenician alphabet system and is related to languages such as Aramaic and Syriac. It is a Semitic language, which means that it was spoken by the descendants of Noah's son, Shem.

Hebrew is written and read from right to left and top to bottom. The main symbols are consonants that have vowel points placed above and below them.

Hebrew consonants are as follows:

Letter	Name	Letter	Name	Letter	Name
א	Alep	ט	Tet	ב ב ף	Pe
ב ב	Bet	י	Yod	צ ץ	Sade
ג ג	Gimel	כ ך ך	Kap	ק	Qop
ד ד	Dalet	ל	Lamed	ר	Res
ה	He	מ ם	Mem	ט ש	Sin, Shin
ו	Waw	נ ן	Nun	ת ת	Taw
ז	Zayin	ס	Samek		
ח	Het	ע	Ayin		

Hebrew vowel points are as follows:

Letter	Name	Letter	Name
ֲ	Pathah	ָ	Qames
ֱ	Seghol	ֳ	Hatuph
ִ	Hireq	ֻ	Qibbus

These combine to form Hebrew words, such as:

Ădônây	Lord	אֲדֹנָי
yehwah	Lord	יְהוָה
ʾâhab	to love	אָהַב
rûwach	spirit	רוּחַ
shâchâh	to worship	שָׁחָה
nephesh	soul	נֶפֶשׁ

Multilingual Word Processor Software

CHIWRITER is a multilingual and scientific word processor that was designed by Cay Horstmann, who created the program to help him with his thesis. It is a WYSIWYG word processor that is capable of working both with foreign languages and mathematical/scientific formulas.

The program offers a standard set of text processing features, including editing, saving, printing, formatting, search and replace, and related features. Some of the unique features of this program are its wide range of fonts, a font designer, and ease in transferring back and forth between different fonts.

The fonts available include standard English text, script, Gothic, orator text for headings, foreign font for European languages such as French, German, and Spanish (complete with umlauts, accents, and other special symbols), a symbol font (copyright, trademark, paragraph, etc.), a Greek letter font, and linedraw fonts. Two math fonts include such symbols as integrals, summation, square roots, products, and curly braces.

The Greek and Hebrew fonts allow the user to create Greek with accents and breathing marks, as well as Hebrew in either biblical or modern typeface. The program supports WYSIWYG vowel points in the Hebrew fonts.

MULTILINGUAL SCHOLAR. If you are looking for a comprehensive DOS multilingual word processor that supports dozens of languages, this is certainly a package to consider. The program provides a full range of word processing features including search and replace, word wrap, blocks, importing of text, and extensive formatting features (headers, footers, superscripts, subscripts, footnotes, columns, margins, line spacing, font changes, and page size).

The program provides access to all the Greek letters, as well as vowels and accents. Hebrew is presented right to left and all the vowels, half vowels, dipthongs, and other components of words can be created with a few keystrokes (single keys, or combinations of keys). One advantage of this program is the ability to combine text in different languages, even on the same line. Thus, segments of text in Greek or Hebrew can have English commentaries added beside them.

Other features of the program include print preview, which lets the user see on the screen what a document will look like when it is printed in different sizes ranging from part of the page to the entire page. In addition, a font generator module lets the user create new fonts, modify existing fonts, and make other kinds of changes such as adding new letters. While there are preset keyboard layouts for each language that map the English keyboard to corresponding foreign characters or alphabets, the program also lets the user modify the different layouts according to personal preference.

The program includes five alphabets: Roman (English and Western European languages), Hebrew, Greek, Cyrillic (Russian and Eastern European), and Arabic. Aside from these, many other languages are available as add-on packages. Some of the languages come with optional fonts as well.

The program works with both dot-matrix printers and various models of laser printers.

PC HEBREW WRITER. This low-cost multilingual word processor works exclusively with Hebrew and English. Its standard word processing features include search and replace, blocks, justification, word wrap, and more.

UNIVERSE FOR WINDOWS. This program provides access to many different languages, including Greek and Hebrew, and uses the graphical capabilities of Microsoft Windows. It was designed to create foreign words easily, even those that are complex in structure. It offers "transparent" support for all languages that are included, which means that any of the languages can be mixed in a document, even on the same line. In addition, the program automatically sets up the text in the proper format, with left to right for English and other Western European languages, right to left for Hebrew, and up and down for languages such as Chinese and Japanese.

The program features spell checking for multiple foreign languages including simultaneous checking of several languages within one document.

A LanguageLink feature provides the capability to use left-to-right languages in many Windows applications. Other features of the program include the availability of pull-down menus, toolbars, and use of the mouse. The user can cut and paste text between different document windows on the screen, whether they be windows of the same or different documents.

This program comes with complete print support that produces high-quality printouts on all Windows supported printers. The program follows the Unicode character encoding standard, which means the program can work with complex languages as easily as with English. All of the foreign language texts, no matter how complex, are displayed on the screen in their complete form, and printouts are reproductions of what appears on the screen.

The basic package comes with English and all major Western and Eastern European languages, together with Greek, Hebrew, Hindi, Chinese, and a bonus of both an optional language and a spell checker/hyphenation add-on disk.

Review of Font and Other Related Software

The programs just described are full featured and provide a wide range of capabilities in both the Greek and Hebrew languages, as well as in English. In addition to these programs, there are other programs that do not have a full range of features, but they do provide the capability of working with Greek and Hebrew language fonts.

SCRIPTURE FONTS. For those who want to work with Greek or Hebrew, but do not want or need to change to a full multilingual word processor, this program would be helpful. It allows the user to work with the original biblical languages using Word Perfect versions 5.0 and 5.1.

WORDPERFECT HEBREW and **WORDPERFECT GREEK.** These programs allow the user to work with either Hebrew or Greek from within Word Perfect 5.1. These add-on packages provide all the capabilities of WordPerfect, as well as the ability to create documents in Hebrew or Greek as well as in Hebrew or Greek and English.

Languages that are Available on Various Multilingual Word Processors

Asian Languages: Burmese, Chinese (traditional and simplified), Indian (different dialects), Korean, Lao, Mongolian, Thai, Tibetan, Vietnamese, Japanese

Eastern European Languages: Albanian, Bulgarian, Byelorussian, Croatian, Czech, Estonian, Hungarian, Latvian, Lithuanian, Macedonian, Polish, Romanian, Russian, Serbian, Slovak, Slovenian, Ukrainian

Western European: Danish, Dutch, French, Finnish, German, Italian, Norwegian, Portuguese, Spanish, Swedish

Mediterranean/Middle Eastern/African Languages: Arabic, Armenian, Ethiopian, Georgian, Greek, Hebrew, Pashto, Persian, Turkish, Urdu

In Closing

If you are preparing a sermon, a scholarly paper, or a Greek/Hebrew language lesson, it would be helpful to be able to write text in Greek or Hebrew and print it out. You can do this with a multilingual word processor.

There are a number of these specialized programs on the market, and they not only provide many of the standard word processing features available in English-based programs, but they also provide the ability to create, view, and print out Greek,

Hebrew, and other languages in their full character form. While most of these programs must be purchased separately, there are a few Bible searching programs that have built-in multilingual word processors.

While these programs are not for everyone, those individuals who work extensively with biblical (and foreign) languages to create papers, theses, scholarly books, and Greek/Hebrew lessons, who want the capability to work with both the original languages and English, will find a multilingual word processor to be a productive and invaluable tool.

Chapter Six

The Electronic Sermon:

Sermon and Bible Lesson Resources

"Preach the word."
2 Timothy 4:2 (KJV)

On a given Sunday morning when you are ushered into the church sanctuary to hear the morning message, one of the thoughts uppermost in your mind is likely to be: I hope this sermon will be exciting, inspiring, and meaningful. And if you are the one who has carefully prepared that sermon and you are about to deliver it, your thoughts will probably be the same—I hope this sermon is exciting, inspiring, and meaningful!

The quality of a sermon is judged not only by the subject of the message and the facts presented but also by how effectively the message reaches out and touches its audience. In this regard, the use of illustrations, quotations, narration, and facts can make a message more effective. These elements add a sense of life, vitality, and realism to a sermon or Bible lesson. As Haddon W. Robinson discussed in his book, *Biblical Preaching*, well-chosen, effective illustrations are good for validating, explaining, and applying ideas and can help to render truths believable.

The goal of this chapter is to present various software programs that can be used to prepare sermons and Bible lessons. Most of these programs focus on methods for using and managing Bible illustrations and related information. Other programs are designed to assist in coordinating hymns and music with the message.

Sermon Resources

Preparing an effective sermon is a multistep process. According to Haddon Robinson, these steps include: (1) selecting the passage, (2) studying the passage, (3) discovering and analyzing the exegetical idea, (4) formulating the homiletical idea, (5) determining what is the purpose of the sermon and how to accomplish it, (6) creating and developing an outline, and (7) finishing up the sermon.

While computer Bible software can assist in many of the stages listed above, one area in particular where software can help is with sermon illustrations. In the following pages we will discuss programs to help in creating sermons and lessons, beginning with helps for illustrations. Other programs assist with outlining and planning a sermon or lesson, and organizing music; they also provide word processing. With help from these tools you can be on your way to a better, more dynamic sermon in no time at all.

AUTOILLUSTRATOR. This program is designed to function as an electronic filing cabinet for preachers. It could be called an illustration management system because it can be used with one or more illustration files.

Featuring graphical-based screens and pull-down menus, the program stores multiple illustrations in a compact, electronic form that eliminates the need for paper files and filing cabinets. With this large database the user can search for illustrations relevant to topics and subtopics because all of these illustrations have been extensively cross-referenced, a tremendous help when you want to find a specific illustration on a broad topic such as love. The program allows for searches of words and combinations of words in the text—in the latter case using Boolean search operators (AND, OR, NOT). An additional intuitive search facility allows the user to add several subtopics together in order to create a narrow, focused search.

The program is designed to work effectively with large numbers of illustration items—as many as 10,000 illustrations cross-referenced 47,000 times, by some 200 topics. In addition to searches, it is also possible to add personal illustrations, edit existing material, tag illustrations with information such as date and place used, and add personal cross-references and topics.

One advantage of the AUTOILLUSTRATOR is that all of the illustrations from its wide selection are royalty-free. They are available either as separate files or as packages with several preloaded files. For instance, you can purchase a package that contains the approximately 1,580 illustrations found in Michael P. Green's book, *Illustrations for Biblical Preaching*. You can also obtain files on leadership and a set of parables and stories.

BIBLE ILLUSTRATOR. If you're looking for illustrations, quotes, anecdotes, and news items to use in your sermon or lesson, this program can help. There are more than 2,500 illustrations in this package, and you can add more either by entering your own or by receiving updates through a quarterly subscription service.

The program features a friendly, graphical interface, complete with pull-down menus. It indexes the items, so the user can search for them by word, phrase, topic, or subtopic. Once an illustration is found, it can be viewed on the screen, printed out, and edited using a built-in mini word processor. Also, illustrations can be saved to ASCII files to be used with other programs and word processors. The program also maintains a usage history for each illustration card and records the last date an illustration was used. Illustrations are keyed to topics in the Thompson Chain Reference Bible and are provided by Sermons Illustrated, a service that routinely provides this information on index cards.

INFOSEARCH. NavPress Software has produced a line of message preparation tools that enable the user to gather, organize, and access supporting materials for sermons, speeches, and other presentations. This series, called INFOSEARCH, comes with five separate databases: Sermon Illustrations, Humor Collection, Current Thoughts and Trends, Hymnal for Worship and Celebration, and Hosanna! Music Praise and Worship. The last two databases, which focus on music, allow the user to keep a database of hymns and songs that are relevant to the theme and message of a service.

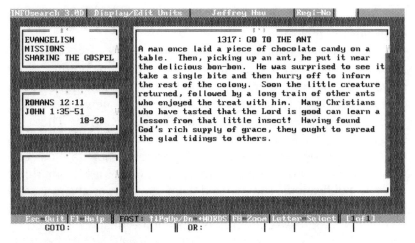

EVANGELISM
MISSIONS
SHARING THE GOSPEL

ROMANS 12:11
JOHN 1:35-51
18-20

1317: GO TO THE ANT
A man once laid a piece of chocolate candy on a table. Then, picking up an ant, he put it near the delicious bon-bon. He was surprised to see it take a single bite and then hurry off to inform the rest of the colony. Soon the little creature returned, followed by a long train of other ants who enjoyed the treat with him. Many Christians who have tasted that the Lord is good can learn a lesson from that little insect! Having found God's rich supply of grace, they ought to spread the glad tidings to others.

Fig. 6.1 A sermon illustration. (Courtesy of NavPress.)

With the advanced features of this INFOSEARCH program, such as indexing, cross-referencing, and cross-linking, it is easy to find an exact illustration, story, anecdote, and musical piece. Simply type in a search term such as a topic, Scripture reference, or word and the program will select the appropriate item.

The latest version of the program, version 3, also features text compression, a "find" function, and a more friendly user interface. The text compression makes it possible to store more illustrations in less space (saving valuable room on the hard disk), and the "find" function retrieves information by locating words used in the desired illustrations or items.

One of the INFOSEARCH databases, Sermon Illustrations, comes complete with more than two thousand indexed sermon illustrations that are cross-referenced by subject, Scripture reference, and key words. The user can take advantage of the filing/indexing system to manage sermon illustration stories, to edit an illustration file, or to add personal examples. Although a vast number of illustrations are provided, new ones can be obtained through the quarterly *Illustrations* update supplement.

If you are interested in adding humor to your messages, talks, and lessons, the Humor Collection program can help you. It is an INFOSEARCH database of well over two thousand jokes, stories, and anecdotes that are indexed by topic and Scripture reference for easy search and retrieval. The text for this program is based on such humor books as *The Treasury of Clean Jokes*, the *Treasury of*

Clean Church Jokes, The Treasure of Clean Jokes for Children, and other titles in this series.

One of the challenges of preparing timely, up-to-date sermons is the need to search out, collect, and organize articles and news items of current interest. And it is a job that must go on continuously in order to stay abreast of the latest news and trends. While this may seem like an exhausting job, Current Thoughts and Trends is a database in the INFOSEARCH system that can do this work for you. An editorial team at Navpress Software has collected relevant articles and newspaper clippings from thirty different publications, summarized them into concise abstracts, and then stored them in an indexed database. This program provides access to an impressive amount of current information indexed by author, publication, subject, Scripture reference, and bibliographic details. The package includes a year's worth of abstracts, as well as one subsequent update. Future updates are available on a quarterly basis through a subscription.

ILLUSTRATION FINDER. Voicings Publications provides a number of products that are useful to pastors who are engaged in the process of creating sermons. This includes the two computerized sermon programs (ILLUSTRATION FINDER and SERMONWARE) as well as two printed publications, *The Preacher's Illustration Service,* a bimonthly printed series of Bible illustrations, and *Sunday Sermons,* a bimonthly edition of full-text sermons.

ILLUSTRATION FINDER is a computerized system for managing and accessing Bible illustrations. The user can search for and view the illustrations on the screen, can print them out, edit them, and even transfer the text to a word processor. The illustrations are indexed by Scripture reference, as well as by topics and subtopics. Users can add new entries into the database. The program comes with about one thousand stories and anecdotes, and current updates can be obtained on a daily basis.

SERMONWARE. If you are looking for an effective sermon on a subject, but cannot seem to come up with the exact message yourself, SERMONWARE could serve as an added resource. This program provides the full text of 328 sermons on computer disk through the SERMONWARE program. The sermons come in two separate volumes and include two sermons for every Sunday, making up a three-year lectionary cycle plus sermons for Christmas, Good Friday, and New Year's Day.

THE NEW BIBLE LIBRARY. THE NEW BIBLE LIBRARY is a CD-ROM based program that provides a range of Bible study tools including Bibles, word study guides, commentaries, and dictionaries. In addition, it provides three thousand sermon-related items, including sermons, outlines, and illustrations. These are broken down into six separate sections, including Basic Bible Truths, Children's Sermons, Evangelistic Sermons, Gospel Sermons, Christian Life, and Gospel Illustrations. In order to use these, you need to have a CD-ROM drive and the appropriate software.

Bible Lesson Planners

LESSON MAKER. One of the basic steps in planning a group study is to find an appropriate subject and lesson plan for the group that will be studying the lesson. While there are many predesigned studies available, they may or may not be exactly suitable for the needs of the study group. As an alternative, the LESSON MAKER program is designed to facilitate the entire process of developing a customized lesson.

There are roughly eighteen thousand questions in the lesson planner database categorized into four phases of a lesson. For example, Open It provides questions for warm up discussions, Explore It for observation questions, Get It for interpretive questions, and Apply It for application discussions. The questions can be used as they are, or they can be modified. If you do not have the time to go through the process of developing your own lesson, you can use the predesigned studies that are part of the program.

Music Software

HYMNAL FOR WORSHIP AND CELEBRATION. Designed to help pastors or worship leaders integrate music with the sermon, this program is a computerized database of hymns indexed according to approximately twenty topics and fifty Scripture references. A quick search will retrieve the exact hymns to coordinate with a particular message. If you have a sound board, with a few keystrokes the computer will even play the hymns!

HOSANNA! MUSIC PRAISE AND WORSHIP. Hymns and choruses are an important part of the Christian church service. This helpful program allows the user to access a complete collection of the Hosanna! Music (R) series (books 1-5, and tapes 3-36). The praise and worship songs in this series, taken largely from Scripture, are sometimes referred to as the "new hymns." These songs are indexed by Scripture reference, topic, title, musical key, tempo, and recording of first release. You can use this program to search for songs based on any of these categories and put together medleys and appropriate musical programs to match your services and sermons.

Word Processing

Thus far we have discussed how specialized computer programs can help users to prepare better sermons, lessons, and music programs. Word processing is another valuable tool to use in preparing sermons and lessons, especially with regard to presentation, format, grammar, and spelling.

Actually, a word processor is one of the most helpful tools for preparing sermons and lessons. More than simply an electronic typewriter, this software package allows the user to actually process words, to manipulate them, to change them, to print them in various formats, check for misspellings and grammatical errors, and merge files of words together. More powerful programs are being introduced all the time, and even a basic program will save hours of retyping and manual correction.

In simplest terms, working with a text document in electronic form not only allows for greater flexibility, it also speeds up the process of development and formatting. With a word processor you can insert text, delete text, change information on the screen, move text from one part of a document to another or even to an entirely different document, search for (and replace) words within a document, set tabs, and even see more than one text document on the screen at once. When you are finished working with a document you can save a copy of it to your disk, where it is stored until the next time you want to work with it.

Another strength of a word processor is its ability to help the user format text properly. This includes setting margins, formatting paragraphs to various forms of justification (lining up one or both sides of a paragraph), printing page numbers, and using different typefaces and fonts both onscreen and in printing out the document.

Other advantages of using a word processor include spell checking and grammar checking, which evaluates a manuscript for general grammar, punctuation, word usage, cliches, and the like. Some word processors also have electronic thesaurus programs that suggest synonyms for words in the document and other functions that help to create indexes, footnotes, and bibliographies.

People who change from typing to word processing soon discover the amazing ease and flexibility of working with computerized documents. No longer do they have to retype a page due to errors, or use whiteout and correction tape. No longer do they have to undergo the tedious process of typing information into the text of a sermon or lesson. Instead, they use the word processor to export material, whether a verse, chapter, or longer text, from computerized Bible and sermon programs.

Some of the major word processing programs on the market include MICROSOFT WORD (for both DOS and Windows), WORDPERFECT (both DOS and Windows versions), AMI PRO, XYWRITE, and others. The best way to start using a word processor is to purchase one that best meets your needs and fits within your budget. Then read through the manual, tutorial, and instruction books, and proceed according to the directions one step at a time. Although some of the processes may seem bewildering at first, they will become clear as you move through the individual steps. It can also be helpful to take a course in word processing if one is offered in your area.

In Closing

Preparing sermons, speeches, and lessons is a big job, from initially researching and collecting relevant illustrations and anecdotes to arranging it all in an organized format. But you do not have to rely solely on your own capabilities to do this job! There are numerous computer programs designed to provide searchable databases of sermon illustrations, to do research using periodical search programs, to provide access to the complete text of sermons, and to aid in coordinating music with sermons. Then when you want to format the material you have gathered, there are efficient, time-saving word processors to make the process easy and enjoyable.

While there is no computer program guaranteed to produce a perfect sermon, there are computer programs and aids available to help make yours as interesting and inspiring as possible.

Chapter Seven

Library on a Disk:
CD-ROM Study Resources

> *". . . of making many books*
> *there is no end."*
> *Ecclesiastes 12:12 (KJV)*

alk into the office of any pastor or professor of theology and you are likely to see a vast array of reference works arranged neatly on bookshelves around the walls. There are volumes of every conceivable kind—Bibles, commentaries, Bible encyclopedias, lexicons, concordances, and word study guides. For centuries printed books have been one of the basic mediums of recording and receiving biblical knowledge.

That is, until now. Today we can benefit from a totally new way of working with biblical information. The typical book of printed pages and glossy dust jackets has taken on a new shape—a collection of microscopic bits of information stored on a computer disk five inches in diameter and weighing just a few ounces. One of these small disks, called a CD-ROM (Compact-Disk Read-Only Memory), can hold the equivalent of an entire shelf of books, or in the neighborhood of 250,000 to 300,000 pages of text! Not only is the sheer size of the data mind boggling, but so is the speed at which the data can be accessed.

Although CD-ROMs have been available for some time, because of their prohibitive prices they have been used mainly in libraries or by large institutions. Recently, however, the technology and the market for CD-ROMs have developed to the point where individuals can now buy both a CD-ROM player and CD-ROM disks at reasonable prices. Any student of Scripture can have personal access to an entire library of useful information, including computerized encyclopedias, dictionaries, commentaries, and other reference texts.

Anyone interested in studying the Bible can benefit from the wealth of information that is so easily accessible from the CD-ROM Bible resource products on the market. In this chapter we will explain the CD-ROM technology, then we will discuss the benefits of the technology, and, finally, we will provide an overview of some of the CD-ROM products that are currently available.

The Expanding World of CD-ROMs

The CD-ROM disk is distinct from a floppy disk in that it may be read from but not written on. The information on these disks is nonvolatile, unerasable, yet immediately available at all times. The technology behind the development of these disks is impressive. A single disk consists of a spiral of pits and marks three miles long. A laser beam reads these pits and translates them into information that the computer can understand. The average capacity of a CD-ROM is in the neighborhood of five hundred to seven hundred megabytes (millions of characters). Compare this to a floppy disk that holds only 1.5 megabytes. THE BIBLE LIBRARY, a CD-ROM biblical library, has the equivalent of 50,000 pages of text encompassing 31 reference volumes on a single CD-ROM disk. In print these volumes would weigh over one hundred pounds!

The vast amount of information that can be stored on a single CD-ROM disk is staggering, yet that is what makes it ideal as a biblical research resource. Imagine the hours of research that can be saved by utilizing one of these programs to search its database and within seconds to produce pages and pages of information that, with the printed volumes, would have taken hours to find and record.

Computer products such as CD-ROM programs provide new and improved means of obtaining information. One of the main disadvantages of printed resources is that they are static and linear, that is the information must generally be obtained by progressing along a line of development from point A to point B to point C and so forth. But educators tells us that, in reality, people rarely think or reason in a strictly linear or one dimensional way. Rather, the human mind moves from a basic topic to subtopics to related topics and back to the basic topic in a multidimensional fashion. This is where the CD-ROM disks are advantageous, because the data in the disk has been organized using hypertext principles, which means the material is presented in categories and is linked by topic, subtopic, etc. This allows the user to start with a general topic and to immediately proceed to deeper levels of the topic or to move to related topics or subtopics as he or she desires.

How a CD-ROM Works

A CD-ROM is a small plastic disk that holds a large amount of information. Data is stored on a CD-ROM on a long, spiral track that runs from the outer edges to the center. While most computer disk drives always spin at the same rate, CD-ROM drives slow down when the detector (reader laser) reads closer to the center of the disk, thus allowing more data to be stored on the disk compared to magnetic floppy disks.

Unlike the magnetic signals of floppy diskettes, CD-ROM drives use light to read information off of the disks. Thus, a main component of a CD-ROM disk drive is the detector, which focuses a concentrated beam of light onto the underside of a CD-ROM disk. The laser beam travels through the disk's protective layer of plastic and strikes the shiny, metallic bottom layer of the disk. This metallic layer contains lands, or flat surfaces, and pits, which are raised portions. The lands and pits represent the 1s and 0s of the data. Light that hits a land is reflected back into the detector, while light that hits a pit is scattered. The light that hits a land will create small electrical voltages that, together with a timing circuit, create a stream of 1s and 0s for the computer to interpret.

Source: White, R., *How Computers Work*, ZD Press, 1993.

Necessary Equipment

Getting started with CD-ROM programs is not as difficult as many people think. All that is necessary is a CD-ROM drive and the associated software.

Let's start with CD-ROM drives. These compact drives are either installed into the body of the computer or are set up as separate, external units. Once installed, the internal CD-ROM drive becomes part of the computer, much like an additional floppy drive—an arrangement that saves desktop space. External drives, on the other hand, must be hooked up to the computer with cables and a plug-in circuit board.

Once the CD-ROM drive hardware is installed, the driver software and a special program known as MSCDEX (Microsoft CD-ROM Extensions) will need to be activated if the drive is being used on a PC under the DOS operating system. This program allows the user to access the CD-ROM drive just like any other floppy disk drive. CD-ROM drives can also be used with Microsoft Windows and with the Apple Macintosh.

Although at first glance the manual for a CD-ROM drive, with its myriad of terms and new concepts, can seem bewildering, the process of actually working with a CD-ROM drive is not difficult at all. In fact, many drives come with a disk that contains all the necessary drivers and programs. These can be installed simply by running an installation program that sets everything up on the hard drive automatically. Once the hardware and the program are in place, the next step is to insert the CD-ROM disk into the disk driver, and the program is ready to use.

Now, what do these programs provide? Plenty!

CD-ROM Bible Reference Libraries

While Bible-related CD-ROMs are not as numerous as the dozens of secular CD-ROMs that are flooding the marketplace these days, there are still many to choose from. Anyone who is interested in studying the Bible in depth will be pleased with what is presently available.

Most of the Bible-related CD-ROM packages currently on the market are devoted entirely to Bible study. Representing Bible texts, Bible reference books, and other resources, these programs are impressive not only because of the number of reference sources they provide, but because of their powerful capabilities to work with this data.

Below is a brief overview of four of the most useful CD-ROM programs on the market and a synopsis of how the capabilities of the programs can be used in Bible study. The resources mentioned in this chapter are designed to be affordable for individuals and small organizations. While some of the CD-ROM products are priced in the hundreds of dollars, they are still considered reasonable in light of the value of the resources they contain.

CD WORD LIBRARY. Developed in conjunction with the Dallas Theological Seminary of Dallas, Texas, this program is a comprehensive resource consisting of Bible translations and original texts, Greek lexicons, Bible dictionaries, commentaries, theological dictionaries, and various charts, maps, and illustrations—all contained on one CD-ROM disk.

Like having a library of Bible resources in the palm of the hand, this program provides capabilities for everything from reading passages in the Bible to performing in-depth biblical studies. It comes complete with a runtime version of Microsoft Windows (version 2.0), which allows access to the information using a graphical-user interface and is menu-driven so it can be used with a mouse. This program enables the user to study parallel Bible texts and commentaries together on the screen at once. In addition, the texts can be presented in a synchronized fashion so the passage in an English translation is displayed in one window, the passage in original Greek is displayed right next to it, and in yet another window the commentary for the passage is displayed. This allows for fast and efficient comparisons between versions, texts, and comments, completely eliminating the time-consuming process of shifting back and forth between multiple Bibles, commentaries, and other resources.

The Greek New Testament and Septuagint in this program provide automatic parsing for every Greek word. Other resources include maps, charts, diagrams, and graphical illustrations.

The CD WORD LIBRARY provides English translations of the Bible, Greek texts, lexicons, dictionaries, and commentaries. English translations include the *King James Version, New International Version, New American Standard Bible,* and *Revised Standard Version.*

In terms of Greek texts, the disk provides the *Septuagint* (LXX), and the Nestle-Aland Greek New Testament, *Novum Testamentum Graece.* Greek Lexicons included in the program are the Bauer, Arndt, Gingrich, and Dankar lexicon, *A Greek-English Lexicon of the New Testament and Other Early Christian Literature,* the intermediate *A Greek-English Lexicon* by H. Liddell and R. Scott, and the *Theological Dictionary of the New Testament* (TDNT) by G. Kittel and G. Friedrich.

There are several other Bible references, including the *New Bible Dictionary* (IVP; 1980) and *Harper's Bible Dictionary* (Harper and Row; 1985). The program also includes several commentaries such as *Harper's Bible Commentary* (Harper and Row; 1988), both the Old and New Testament volumes of *The Bible Knowledge Commentary* (Victor; 1985, 1983), and the *Jerome Biblical Commentary* (Prentice-Hall; 1968).

The features of the CD WORD LIBRARY that make it a highly useful resource are: (a) powerful hypertext-based structuring and searching capabilities, (b) window-based user interface, and (c) advanced techniques for working with biblical Greek.

What can be accomplished with these resources? As a start, the program can be used to compare various Bible translations using different windows. This procedure makes it possible to compare Luke 8, for example, in the Revised Standard Version and the New American Standard Bible. This comparison indicates that in verse 6, NASB uses the words *rocky soil* while RSV uses *rock*. In verse 10, NASB mentions *mysteries* while RSV uses *secrets*. The program can also be used to locate and view Bible references that contain specific words (word searches) through the pull-down menu system. This capability includes finding verses where several words occur together or where one of a number of words (such as synonyms) are used.

With this program it is simple to do phrase searches such as "Son of Man" or "Kingdom of Heaven," and to find verses that contain two separate words such as *sower* and *seed*. The program also features wildcard options: the multi-character wildcard (*) **"sower*"** would retrieve such matches as "sower" and "sowers" (the number of characters beyond the * is not limited), and the single-character wildcard (?) as in **seed?** will produce the matches "seed," "seeds," and "seedy" (the number of characters after the ? is limited to one).

The program also allows for proximity searches. This enables the user to determine how far one word can be separated from other words. For instance, the search term **sower near_3_verses see** would look for any chapter in the Bible where both of these words occur, but the words must be three or fewer verses apart.

The request can be even more specific. For example, **"god" before_5_words almighty** would search for all verses where *god* occurs five words before *almighty*.

The OR command feature locates verses that match any one of several loosely related words, such as **simple* OR fool* OR glutton***. A search operator specifies certain words while others are excluded. For instance, **("Jesus" OR "Lord") OR ("ship" OR "boat") NOT "disciple*"** will exclude those verses containing the word *disciple* (or a variation of it) from the list of verses that have Jesus or Lord, or ship or boat.

In addition to multiple search capabilities, this program can be used to locate background information on a wide variety of topics through *Harper's Bible Dictionary* (HBD) and the *New Bible Dictionary* (NBD). *Harper's Bible Dictionary*, edited by Paul Achtemeier (1986), gives a comprehensive coverage of important Bible subjects and topics from Aaron to Zurishaddai. Over 179 contributors wrote entries that represent a nonsecretarian consensus view of each subject.

The *New Bible Dictionary*, edited by J. D. Douglas, contains the work of over 150 scholars from around the world. It covers a wide range of knowledge about people, places, and books of the Bible, words of the Bible, doctrines, history, geography, and culture. The information is written in a style that is highly informative and yet easy to read.

These computerized dictionaries can be used in several different ways. They can be accessed from words within Bible translations, from a specific topic that is selected for review, or from a topic that is chosen from a cross-reference. For example, a study can be initiated with the word *boat,* which appears in the computerized text of Matthew 13:2; it can be initiated simply by entering the topic *boat* directly onto the screen; or it can commence with the entry *boat* and then proceed to another cross-reference such as *Egypt*.

This program also provides a set of pictures, diagrams, and maps including graphical diagrams (maps) of the route of the Exodus and of the land of Canaan during the time of the Judges. These can be viewed onscreen and can be printed out in a hard copy.

The five different commentary volumes that are available provide detailed information on whatever verse is selected. These commentaries differ in several ways. The *Bible Knowledge Commentary* was developed by the Dallas Theological Seminary and provides an easy-to-understand analysis of paragraphs and verses of the New International Version (NIV). It provides detailed information about each book of the Bible including the author, purpose, historical background, outline, commentary on each verse, and a bibliography. This information includes comments on problem passages, customs, geography, and important words, along with pertinent maps and diagrams.

Harper's Bible Commentary provides information on the Bible in three distinct formats: (1) general articles on the Bible as a whole (culture, literary context, historical background), (2) reports discussing books with significant relationships to each other, and (3) commentaries on each of the individual books. This commentary is written for general audiences.

The *Jerome Biblical Commentary* is designed for Catholic readers with an emphasis on interpretation of the Scriptures. General articles discuss topics of history and geography, as well as recent discoveries regarding the Apocryphal Gospels and the Dead Sea Scrolls.

Since all of these commentaries are indexed by passage or verse, the user can choose the specific portion of Scripture to be studied. For instance, to find out what the *Bible Knowledge Commentary* says about Matthew 13, the user would simply key in this text, and the program would display both the original text and the commentary notes side-by-side on the screen.

Among the most outstanding features of the CD WORD LIBRARY are the tools it provides to work with Scripture texts in the original Greek. The program provides both original Greek texts and a set of lexicons. The Nestle-Aland Greek New Testament is available, as well as Rahlf's *Septuagint* (LXX).

Moving from the Greek to the English and vice versa is a simple process with these tools, which is what makes them so valuable. For instance, simply clicking on a word in the New American Standard Bible (NASB) translation activates the program to display both the corresponding Greek New Testament verse and the specific Greek word (or words).

This linking between the NASB and the Greek text simplifies the process of understanding the original Greek word(s) behind the English translation. For example, suppose we had the verse Matthew 13:3 on our screen and we selected the word *sower* for our study. Not only would this program tell us that the Greek word is σπείρω (*speiro*), it would also provide the definition of the word from any one of the three lexicons that we chose: the Bauer, Arndt, Gingrich, and Dankar *Lexicon of Koine Greek*, the Liddell and Scott *Lexicon of Classical Greek*, or the single volume edition of *The Theological Dictionary of the New Testament* (TDNT).

Another useful feature of the Greek program is its ability to automatically parse a Greek word. For example, we find the word ἐκαυματίση (*ekaumatistha*) in Matthew 13:6 in the Greek New Testament. By selecting the parser feature, we learn that the word means "to burn up," that it has the root or lexical form καυματίζω (*kaumatizō*), and that it is a third person, singular, aorist, passive, and indicative verb. The system not only performs the tedious task of parsing the word, but also provides the root and an approximate meaning.

With this system the user can also search directly in Greek by changing to the Greek mode and typing in the selected Greek word (in Greek letters). The program can search for verses that match a specific form of a Greek word, such as a particular tense and person of a verb, and it can find all instances of a specified word regardless of its category, case, gender, tense, mood, and other factors.

The CD WORD LIBRARY program has many other features, too numerous to explain here, that make it an invaluable resource for serious Bible study. Despite its scholarly orientation, the program is useful to both beginning and advanced Bible students. Logos Research, which is now handling the marketing, distribution, and further development of the program, is planning to release a new version with more up-to-date user interface screens and various other enhancements. (Logos Research can provide further information on these updates.)

THE BIBLE LIBRARY. Another exhaustive resource for Bible study is a CD-ROM product called THE BIBLE LIBRARY. As the name implies, this program provides a library of biblical reference books combined with powerful search and retrieval facilities.

THE BIBLE LIBRARY disk contains twenty-nine Bible resources, including nine Bibles and twenty reference sources. The information available on this single disk represents fifty-thousand pages of text that would cost over $1,400 in print form. The information encompasses a vast range of Bible study capabilities that are activated by clear search and query commands.

THE BIBLE LIBRARY provides Bible versions, dictionaries, commentaries, and other resource materials. In terms of Bible versions, the program offers the *King James Version*, the *New King James Version*, the *American Standard Version*, the *New International Version*, the *Revised Standard Version*, *The Living Bible*, the *Literal English Translation*, and *The Simple English Bible*.

Other resources include Strong's Greek and Hebrew dictionaries, Vine's *Expository Dictionary of Old and New Testament Words*, as well as Harris' *Theological Wordbook of the Old Testament*. Other Bible dictionaries include Easton's *Illustrated Bible Dictionary*, Elwell's *Evangelical Dictionary of Theology*, and Edersheim's *Life and Times of Jesus the Messiah*. The disk also contains *A Commentary on the Whole Bible* by C. Henry, *Home Bible Study Commentary* by J. Gray, *101 Hymn Stories* by K. Osbeck, and a selection of sermon outlines and illustrations.

THE BIBLE LIBRARY's built-in software enables the user to find information quickly through searches and queries, thus saving tedious hours of searching through printed pages. To begin with, Bible versions can be searched for specific verses in the Bible. The program performs word searches and will locate verses that contain a specified English word or set of words. For instance, if someone wanted to find the exact verse in Genesis that has the words *beginning* and *created* the user would enter the phrase **beginning AND created,** and the system would indicate the verse Genesis 001:001. This kind of search uses what is known as a logical operator to connect two separate words in a search.

As an additional feature, the wildcard symbols will search for words even when the exact form of the word is not known. For example, **begin!** or **creat!** specify only what letters the words must begin with; the endings can vary. This broader search would encompass such words as *begin, beginning, create, creator,* or *created,* to cite some examples.

Citation and word searches on this program are similar to the capabilities of most standard Bible software programs. However, this program's ability to do searches on a number of different sources (Bibles, encyclopedias, other reference works) concurrently is what makes it unique. For instance, with this program it is possible to view the parallel translations of Genesis 1:1 in the KJV, the NKJV, the ASV, The Living Bible Paraphrased, the NIV, and the RSV simultaneously.

Another useful tool in THE BIBLE LIBRARY is the Literal Translation, which ties in Strong's numbers and the Hebrew and Greek dictionary definitions to the words in the Scripture text. Additional information on a specific word can be found in the *Theological Dictionary of the Old Testament* or in Vine's dictionary. The other resources on the disk are searchable in various fields, whether they be a topic (such as when using Bible dictionaries), a verse citation, Strong's or Harris' number, or a chapter heading.

Some of the other key features of this program are the *Simple English Bible* (New Testament), which is a new translation based on the original Greek and Hebrew texts, and the *MicroBible*, an easy-to-read, 3,000-word vocabulary narrative of the Bible designed for young and beginning readers. The program also includes Osbeck's *101 Hymn Stories*, which talks about important hymns and their authors, as well as *Ritchie's Sermon Outlines*, a collection of 2,500 nondenominational sermon outlines and 500 sermon illustrations and stories.

Ellis Enterprises has completed an improved version of THE BIBLE LIBRARY that includes new software from IBM and additional

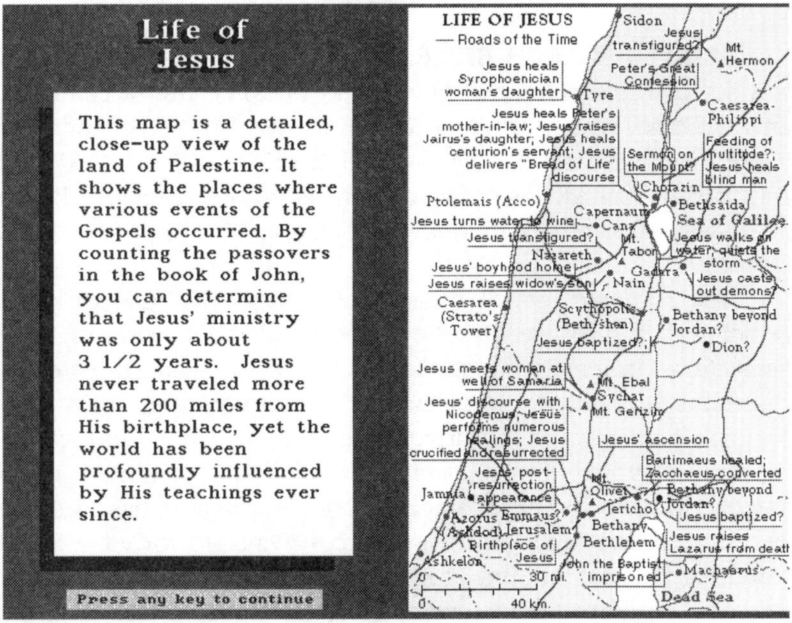

Fig. 7.1 Life of Jesus Map. (Courtesy of Ellis Enterprises.)

reference sources. Called THE NEW BIBLE LIBRARY, this version features faster, improved searches that function simply by highlighting a word or phrase and then clicking on it. The searches are more powerful so a single click produces parallel references in all included versions, as well as cross-references to other included resources. The new Hypersearch! feature simplifies searching for information with a mouse, and a built-in windowing feature allows the program to be run either with Microsoft Windows or DOS. A notepad allows the user to extract information from the various resources, to add personal notes, and to move information to and from the word processor. Other unique features are the bookmark, which records the user's place in each reference work, and a "highlighting pen," which can mark specified verses in the Scriptures.

The additional versions of the Bible in the new program include the *New American Bible with Apocrypha* (Catholic), the *New American Standard Bible*, the *New Jerusalem Version*, Spanish *Reina-Valera Actualizada*, transliterated Bible versions, and the *Chronological Bible*. Additional study resources include Barclay's *Daily Bible Study Series*, Morris' *Introduction to the Bible*, the complete works of Josephus, *Nave's Topical Bible*, and various biblical maps.

MASTER SEARCH BIBLE. Another major CD-ROM product is a set of Bible reference aids called MASTER SEARCH BIBLE. This package, which provides a wide range of Bible versions and reference works, in some ways parallels CD WORD LIBRARY and THE BIBLE LIBRARY in terms of purpose and orientation. But in other ways it offers a unique combination of computerized resources.

The software, which comes on a single CD-ROM disk, together with a software diskette and manual, offers a set of Bible translations, original language texts, as well as several Bible encyclopedias, geography aids, and archaeology references. The program features a menu-driven interface; multiple windows on the screen; word, phrase, or wildcard search capabilities; and a notepad to record personal information. The program has a unique link feature that links all the resources available for ease in researching the vast amount of knowledge in this library.

The program offers several Bible translations, including the *King James Version, New American Standard Version,* and *New*

International Version. It also provides Strong's *Concordance* and two study Bibles: the *NIV Study Bible* and the *Scofield Study Bible.* With regard to associated reference works, this program has the complete text of the *Wycliffe Bible Encyclopedia* (Moody), the *Handbook for Bible Study,* and the *Expository Dictionary of Bible Words* by L. Richards. For Bible background studies, this program offers resources that are unique to this program including *The New Manners and Customs of Bible Times* by R. Gower, the *Wycliffe Historical Geography of Bible Lands* by C. Pheiffer and F. Howard, and *The New International Dictionary of Biblical Archaeology* by D. Blaiklock and R. Harrison.

ABS REFERENCE BIBLE ON CD-ROM. The American Bible Society has produced a CD-ROM version of the Bible known as the ABS REFERENCE BIBLE ON CD-ROM. It provides a wide range of resources, including English language and foreign translations, ancient Bible texts, and various study helps.

The Bible versions contained on the CD-ROM include the *King James Version,* the *Revised Standard Version,* the *New Revised Standard Version,* the *New American Standard Bible,* the *New King James Version,* and *Today's English Version.* Spanish (rva) and German translations (Luther Translation) are also included.

This CD-ROM package is comprehensive in its coverage of ancient Bibles, helps, and study resources, which include the following: *Biblica Hebraica Stuttgartensia* (Hebrew Old Testament), *Greek Septuagint* (Rahlf's Edition), *Latin Vulgate Bible, Greek New Testament* (UBS 3rd edition), *Grammatical Directory of the Hebrew Bible* (Westminster Theological Seminary), *English Translation of the Septuagint* (Branton Edition), *A Grammatical Directory to the Greek New Testament* (GRAMCORD), *A Hebrew Harmony of Samuel-Kings-Chronicles, A Greek Harmony of the Gospels, Morphological Analysis, Computer Assisted Tools for Septuagint Studies* (University of Pennsylvania), *An English Harmony of Samuel-Kings-Chronicles, An English Harmony of the Gospels, The Apostolic Fathers in English* (Lightfoot translation), *The Works of Josephus in English* (Whitson translation), *Dictionary of Bible and Religion* (Abingdon Press).

This is an exhaustive reference source of Scripture and biblical information. The advanced Bible study texts are ideal for those who want to delve deep into Bible study using the original texts and other specialized writings.

In Closing

While the list of CD-ROM products we have included here is by no means exhaustive, it serves as an introduction to the products that are available and provides a glimpse of the expanding capabilities for Bible study and research that such programs provide. We are approaching a new frontier in computer Bible study resources. Gone are the days of dragging around heavy books and flipping through hundreds of pages to find the necessary information. Today, anyone can have an entire library of Bible versions and reference books in one small disk that provides all the information required in a matter of seconds. No longer does Bible study need to be a lengthy, time-consuming process; instead, it can be an adventure with more emphasis placed on interpreting and making new discoveries rather than struggling through tedious time-consuming research. These developments are a positive step in making the truths of the Bible easily accessible to many people, in making Bible study more productive, and in generating excitement for God's word.

Chapter Eight

Dialing for Daniel:
Online Bible Study Resources

*"The heart of the prudent acquires
knowledge, and the ear of the wise
seeks knowledge."*
Proverbs 18:15 *(NKJV)*

S tone tablets were part of the communication system Moses used centuries ago. In Egypt, scholars used hieroglyphics on papyrus sheets to pass information along. In our modern age, we communicate by means of the printed word, the telephone, and now the computer.

Interactive communication by computer is rapidly becoming a viable and accepted form of information exchange. People use electronic mail to send and receive messages, and sophisticated voice-mail systems have replaced answering machines. Faxing memos is in, and using the post office is out! For many people, logging in to a daily computer bulletin board or information source is as routine as reaching for the morning newspaper or opening the daily mail.

With a computer and a telephone line, anyone can have a direct link to a virtually unlimited storehouse of information, larger and more comprehensive than can possibly be imagined. Business and scholarly data are available as are weather reports and the latest news. With these systems it is possible to shop and bank or research the latest information in a chosen area of study—all from the comfort of the chair at your computer desk.

Bible study is one area of research that benefits from the expanding accessibility of online information. Computer communication services, called online services, provide immediate access to the latest theological research. They offer resources for compiling bibliographies and references of biblical information. They offer the ability to debate and converse online with other believers and experts in religion, and they allow access to the latest, up-to-date religious news. These services also include bulletin boards so individuals can share insights and findings with other Christians!

In this chapter we will briefly overview the phenomenon of online communications. We will touch on the hardware and software involved, then we will focus on the various online services that are available for Christians with an emphasis on those that would be most helpful in Bible studies.

Facts about Computer Telecommunications

Computer telecommunications is one of the most exciting developments in computing systems. In a step beyond merely running software programs on the computer, it allows the user to reach out over a telephone wire and make contact with other computers and other users across the nation and around the world.

The Benefits of Computer Telecommunications

What are some of the specific benefits of telecommunicating?

1. **It provides instant access to people and information**. It can be three A.M. in the morning, a blizzard can be raging outside, and yet with computer communications you can still have access to information and ideas. Whether you need to research for a sermon, want to study a particular passage of the Bible, or are curious about a specific biblical subject, telecommunications allows you to reach out, across miles and time, to people and processes for pertinent information.

2. **It expands the power of the computer.** Through telecommunications, thousands of data banks, programs, news reports,

and ideas from individuals are readily available. Like having hundreds of libraries at one's fingertips, telecommunications expands the power and capabilities of an ordinary computer immensely.

3. **It is fast.** Telecommunicating, whether to California, Tokyo, or Paris, happens in a matter of seconds, and costs much less than a comparable long-distance telephone call. It forms an interconnected system between all types of computers, networks, and persons who are scattered throughout the world that operate as though they were in the next room.

4. **It provides selectivity.** The amount of information that is available through telecommunications is enormous—no one individual can use all of it. But whether a person wants the latest religious news or an elusive article on Ecclesiastes, the power of computer searching allows that individual to choose from the available data the exact information that is needed. It is a far cry from the hours that would be spent in a library pouring over printed bibliographies and indexes for the same information.

5. **It is fun.** Interacting with other computer users and corresponding electronically is not only extremely helpful, it is also fun! By means of a telecommunication modem it is possible to travel hundreds of miles to interact with various types of computers (from small home PCs to the world's supercomputers) and to share information and ideas with a variety of people on issues of particular concern. You do not have to study the Bible alone; you can turn on your computer and study online with others.

The Requirements for Computer Telecommunications

Online telecommunication is an exciting, expanding area of computer Bible study that offers many advantages. However, to profit from these study capabilities there are several requirements that must be met:

1. **It requires additional expense.** In order to utilize the system of telecommunications, it is necessary to invest in additional equipment, including a modem, communications software, and perhaps even the cost of a second telephone line. It is also necessary to pay subscription fees for the communication service (though some are available free of charge or for a nominal fee),

telephone charges, and connect time. Depending on the equipment purchased, the volume of usage, as well as the services subscribed to, the costs can range from minimal to high.

Personal needs and interests in telecommunications need to be weighed carefully prior to making the commitment of time and money required for successful computer telecommunications.

2. **It requires a knowledge of and the ability to work with different telecommunications services**. Anyone who has enjoyed the challenge of learning how to use a desktop computer will enjoy learning how to use telecommunications services. Each service varies in its commands, structure, and operation, but with patience and diligence anyone can learn these rather quickly.

Some of the more complex services provide a reference manual of instructions for their system. Obviously, whether brief or lengthy, there will be a necessary learning period for each new system.

3. **It requires some technical knowledge**. While for the most part it is possible to work adequately with a minimum of computer knowledge when using an online Bible, telecommunicating requires a thorough understanding of the technical aspects of computing between systems. These concepts are not difficult, but they do require time and patience to learn.

For instance, it is essential to know how to use a modem and how to formulate communications settings for each service or bulletin board. Thus, you would need to know what an RS-232 interface is, you would need to understand the significance of bps rate, and you would need to know the difference between half and full duplex. Furthermore, you would need to learn how to receive a file from an online service. All of these things—and many more—are pieces of information that are significant to telecommunicating successfully.

Beginning to Communicate

In order to access this electronic universe, it is necessary to modify the standard computer system somewhat. Since telecommunicating ties up the telephone line, it may be desirable to install a second line. The basic piece of hardware that needs to be added is a modem, and, of course, a different kind of software (communications software) is necessary.

The Hardware — A Modem

A modem is a device that turns digital (discrete on-off) signals into analog (continuous sound wave) signals, and vice versa. In other words, the digital signals that your computer reads must be converted into analog signals that can travel through telephone lines. When these analog signals reach their destination, the remote computer's modem will turn them back into digital signals. Without this conversion process the interaction between the two computers across telephone lines would not be possible.

Modems vary in type, baud rate, number of special features, and compatibility to various computers. There are three main types of modems: external, internal, and acoustic.

External modems are units that are maintained outside of the computer system. They are plugged into a communications port in the back of the computer (using cables). These modems come in different speeds, sizes, and with a variety of features.

Internal modems are a type of circuit board that plugs easily into one of the interior computer expansion slots. Like the external models, internal modems can be purchased in a variety of speeds and additional features.

A third type of modem, the **acoustic modem**, while formerly widely used, has become less popular in recent years. Traditionally, these acoustic coupler modems consisted of a rectangular box with two large cups designed to hold the telephone handset. To use it, a computer access number was dialed, and after the carrier tone (signaling the presence of a computer) was received the handset was placed in the coupler. Then incoming data was received through the earpiece and outgoing data was sent through the mouthpiece. Though in limited numbers, some of these modems are still being used, particularly in travel situations where communications can be activated with a standard telephone and a laptop/notebook computer.

The first two categories of modems (internal, external) are referred to as direct-connect modems. They have the advantage of providing better data transmission, and they produce a minimum of distortion; overall their performance is much better than the acoustic coupler modems.

A major consideration when purchasing a modem is speed. The speed of a modem is measured by the terms *baud* and *bits* per second, with the latter, abbreviated as bps, being the more accurate measure. For all practical purposes, 300 bps equals 30 characters per second (cps), 1,200 equals 120 cps, 2,400 equals 240 cps, and so on. Years ago, most modems were designed with 300 or 1,200 bps, but the modems on the market today communicate at speeds such as 2,400, 4,800, 9,600 bps, and even faster.

While the lower speed modems are best for reading information off of a screen, the higher bps modems are ideal for sending and receiving files quickly. As we will discuss in more detail later, one of the basic purposes of having a modem is to receive large amounts of information. However, much of this data can be received as a file and kept for later perusal; it does not have to be read directly off of the screen.

Other modem features that can be selected include easy transference between various modes and speeds, the ability to answer the phone when it rings and establish a connection, the availability of touch tone and pulse dialing, dialing directories, and self-test features. Some of the newer modems also offer Fax (facsimile) sending and receiving processes as part of the unit.

As any modem reference manual will verify, a modem is a complex piece of computer hardware with a bewildering array of codes, modes, and settings—all categorized by strange terms. Since the emphasis in this book is computerized Bible study, we will not discuss further technical details of using a modem. However, there are many helpful books available that explain these intricate concepts and methods for the novice.

The Software

The other important component of computer telecommunications is communications software. Some modems have built-in software, however, the capabilities of these programs are often limited. In general, it is best to purchase a separate communications program that will access the full range of abilities of a modem. These programs perform the complex task of controlling the communications process, not only between the computer and outside systems, but between the user and the modem.

Some of the functions of communications software include controlling the required parameters (settings) of the data that is sent and received, programming the modem to both send and receive data, receiving and sending files of information, storing this information on a disk, maintaining a file of frequently used computer dial-up telephone numbers, and providing other help as needed.

Some of the popular communications software programs include PROCOMM PLUS, SMARTCOM, and CROSSTALK. Sometimes these programs are sold as a package with a modem at a reduced price.

Telecommunications Networks and Services

In order to engage in computer telecommunications it is necessary to establish a connection across telephone lines with another, remote computer. In some cases, this remote computer is accessed through a direct-dial telephone number. This is true for small bulletin boards and local-area services. This connection can be made with a computer as small as a Commodore-64 or as large as an IBM mainframe or Cray supercomputer.

Direct dialing systems are not as good for connections with systems outside the local calling area because long distance telephone charges can quickly mount up. However, large nationwide services (some are mentioned in this chapter) do not expect users to call long distance to access their systems. Instead, they use dial-up networks that provide local call access not only to their system, but to hundreds of others throughout the United States, Canada, and around the world. These networks consist of hundreds of dial-in computer "nodes" located in multiple cities and towns. Any one of these node computers can be accessed through a local phone number.

There are dozens of networks in the United States alone. GTE Sprintnet and McDonnell-Douglas Tymnet are two that are used frequently; there are others run by General Electric, CompuServe, IBM, and ADP. These networks are called packet-switching networks because they send small packets of information back and forth between the nodes and various host computer systems. These networks provide access to computers in distant areas for a comparatively low cost. No matter where you live, there is a network within your reach.

Telecommunications Services — An Overview

Despite a seemingly wide array of services, there are only two main categories of telecommunications services: national commercial services (which generally charge fees), and local free bulletin boards. Commercial services either offer one specific type of information, such as business data, news, bibliographic data, entertainment, etc., or a combination of these. They are professional in quality, are run from large-scale facilities, and charge anywhere from a few dollars to hundreds of dollars per hour. Many of these services charge a subscription fee, an hourly charge, and additional fees for network usage and special services.

The commercial services that are available can be broken down into three main categories: information utilities, professional services, and bibliographic database vendors. Information utilities are basically supermarkets of information that cater to a wide range of audiences. For instance, there are personal services for those who simply want to have some fun or who want to chat with other people on the network; there are professional stock market and business databases available; and there are online conferences for discussions of various topics and information on every imaginable subject. Service companies usually charge a nominal rate for access to the service, with surcharges for the professional and specialized information.

Professional services, such as NewsNet, provide news and specialized data to professionals and persons in specific industries. Because of their exclusivity, these services are generally higher priced than the information utilities.

Finally, bibliographic database vendors provide access to vast quantities of information on a wide variety of subjects usually in the form of references and abstracts from scholarly journals and papers. The prices for these services vary from a few dollars per hour to literally hundreds of dollars per hour.

Bulletin boards, which are typically much smaller in scale, are frequently set up on a single microcomputer or minicomputer. They allow a limited number of users to post bulletins, to join online conferences, to download software, and to send electronic mail to other users. Most electronic bulletin boards are free to callers, with the exception of the long distance call if access is made outside the board's telephone region. Some of these services charge nominal subscriber fees or require that a user call frequently in order to become a full-fledged, validated user.

Services and Applications: News Services

Since telecommunications services can deliver information and data from coast to coast in a matter of seconds, they are ideal for delivering specialized news and newsletters on religious events, subjects, and personalities. Often this information is not available from any other source.

NEWSNET is a primary service for religious news. This vendor offers up-to-the-minute information in the form of highly specialized online newsletters that are released through the service just hours after they are written. It is the ideal service for getting the "inside scoop" on a variety of subjects and business items. Unlike the bibliographic database vendors that provide just a reference and perhaps an abstract, NewsNet provides the full text of the newsletter.

A variety of religious news services are offered by NewsNet including the following:

CHURCH NEWS INTERNATIONAL provides broad coverage of religion around the world, including various events, background, features, and statements about religious groups, churches, and happenings, as well as profiles of various newsworthy religious personalities. Most of the mainline church denominations are covered, as well as ecumenical agencies and both the National and World Council of Churches. The news is updated daily and is recorded as far back as November 3, 1982. It is published by Resources for Communication.

RNS DAILY NEWS REPORTS provides news reports and analyses on religious happenings both in the United States and around the world. It includes comments on how religion interacts with the world community as a whole and how religious events influence social, political, and economic events. This ecumenical news service covers all the mainline church denominations around the world. It is published by the Religious News Service and coverage dates back to August 20, 1984.

LUTHERAN NEWS SERVICE provides detailed information about events in the Lutheran Church of America and the Lutheran World Federation. This includes news of the church's policy statements on various issues, activities both domestic and worldwide, and also relations with other churches. This is a weekly publication.

UNITED METHODIST INFORMATION SERVICE provides news from the United Methodist News Service, as well as related sources including the UM Communicator, the United Methodist Publishing House, the Board of Discipleship, and the Board of Global Ministries. Both news and human-interest items are included in the reports, which are published weekly.

CATHOLIC NEWS SERVICE provides news from the Roman Catholic News Service newswire. It gives broad yet comprehensive coverage of the activities, issues, and happenings of the Roman Catholic Church and its organizations around the world. The information is updated on a daily basis.

CATHOLIC TRENDS discusses church life, policy, education, various ministries, and other areas of interest as they relate to the Roman Catholic Church. The news is published biweekly and dates back to April 1988.

Keep in mind that these religious newsletters are not inexpensive to use. Charges can run as high as $75 or more per hour. Obviously, these are not designed for casual use. However, if you have a specific need for information in one of these areas, NewsNet is a good source.

Services and Applications: In-Depth Christian Information

A bibliographic database, as its name indicates, provides information such as the article, author, title, source, date, and other relevant data. In some cases an abstract or summary of the article is provided. These databases are generally scholarly and serious in nature, and, thus, are not intended for general use. They are appropriate for preparing a paper, an article, or a thesis, or simply to acquire scholarly information for research on a specific subject.

For religious information of a more serious or scholarly nature, the following bibliographic databases would be good sources to use.

The American Theological Library Association has one of the largest collections of religious information in its **ATLA RELIGION**

DATABASE. This one database is actually a package of six separate databases—a virtual powerhouse online religious database. Included in the package are various forms of the *Religion Index*, an *Index to Book Reviews in Religion*, *Research in Ministry*, and *Methodist Reviews Index*.

The RELIGION INDEX ONE (RIO) is a comprehensive database compiled by the American Theological Library Association that is designed for academic and scholarly users. This database, which focuses entirely on religion, indexes thousands of articles on or related to religion, from hundreds of journals. The papers and journals referenced in this database cover every major denomination. RIO is considered to be one of the most complete guides available to current theological thinking.

There are literally hundreds of journals referenced in this database, including such publications as the *Africa Theological Journal, Baptist History and Heritage, Epiphany, Journal of Biblical Literature, Methodist History,* and even the *Indian Journal of Theology and Pastoral Psychology.* You can search a wide selection of topics such as anthropology, art, ecology, law, medicine, and politics as they relate to religion.

There are three different indexes in this database including a subject index, an author-editor index, and a Scripture index, which lists articles that refer to a certain passage of Scripture. The coverage for this database is from 1949 to the present.

A companion to this database is the RELIGION INDEX TWO (RIT), which serves much the same main purpose as RELIGION INDEX ONE; however, rather than periodicals, it indexes books that contain essays and papers related to religion. The focus is on multiauthor scholarly books and includes the three types of indexes mentioned in RIO. This database indexes about 450 books and offers coverage from 1970 to the present. RIO and RIT together comprise one of the largest databases of religious knowledge available. Both are international in scope.

Another part of the ATLA Religion Database is the INDEX TO BOOK REVIEWS IN RELIGION (IBBR), which provides an index to the more than ten thousand book reviews that are published in over five hundred international journals. The source of the reviews range from the *New York Review of Books* to specialized journals such as *Religion* or the *Asbury Theological Journal.* The topics range widely, including bioethics, law, medicine, sociology, and music. There are five different indexes built into the database, including author-editor, book title, series, reviewer, and annual classified. The coverage begins in 1949.

If you are interested in knowing what current research is being done in the field of ministry, you will want to investigate **RESEARCH IN MINISTRY (RIM)**. This database indexes doctoral (D.Min.) theses by subject and author, and provides not only references and order contact information but also abstracts describing each thesis.

For a detailed index to Methodist church literature, look into the **METHODIST REVIEWS INDEX**, which is part of the ATLA Religion Database. The coverage is from 1818 to 1985.

The ATLA Religion Database is available in online form through Dialog Information Services, as well as through CD-ROM and in print form. An abridged form of the database, called **RELIGION INDEXES: RIO/RIT/IBRR 1975-** is available as a subset of the full version with the two religion indexes and the book reviews index.

Services and Applications: Religious Conferences

Aside from acquiring news and in-depth religion information, online telecommunications systems make it possible to discuss, debate, and argue theological subjects in conferences with others. These conferences come under various names: conferences, discussion groups, SIGs (Special Interest Groups), Forums, and the like. Basically, they bring people from different parts of the country (and even the world) into an electronic discussion format to discuss (through computer text input) various subjects and topics of interest. At times these discussions become quite lively, with conflicting viewpoints flying back and forth.

ECUNET, one of the main religion networks in existence today, connects church people throughout the United States and Canada from many different denominations, including Presbyterian, Methodist, Baptist, Roman Catholic, Lutheran, and Anglican.

The service allows users to attend online meetings of different kinds, mainly by reading messages "posted" on the screen by others, responding to them, and then viewing the feedback from other participants. Examples of meetings on the network include Sermonshop, Weekly Psalms, Compassionate Friends, Christian

Century Books, and Spiritual Water. It is also possible to send and receive private electronic mail through this service.

Currently operated from the headquarters of the Presbyterian Church in Louisville, Kentucky, the service can be accessed either by dialing direct to the Presbyterian Church or by dialing through an 800 number. The service is nondenominational.

A monthly fee is charged for unlimited use of the service, and a surcharge is billed for those who want to use the 800 number. BizLink software can automate the sessions on the system.

COMPUSERVE INFORMATION SERVICES provides a Religion Forum for discussing religious topics with other users of the system. There are separate sections for different faiths. Other programs, such as Bible games, are also available through the service.

Services and Applications: Bulletin Boards

One of the best ways to begin working with computer telecommunications is to explore bulletin boards. Because the professional/commercial services are more expensive to use, they are also less frequently used and then only for a definite reason. Christian bulletin boards, on the other hand, are relatively inexpensive and, thus, are frequently accessed simply for personal enjoyment.

Although bulletin boards vary widely in the services they offer, their basic function is to provide electronic bulletin boards where people can "tack up" various messages, ideas, opinions, and news items. A bulletin board system or BBS can have several different bulletin areas running simultaneously, so an individual can enter the particular bulletin that interests him or her the most.

Bulletin boards allow users to read messages posted by other persons, to respond to the messages, and to add personal notes. It is also possible to send and receive electronic mail through the bulletin board systems. In addition, some systems even allow users to download (receive through modem) various programs free of charge, to play games, to carry on a discussion with another user, or simply to sit back and read the information provided by the system and other users.

Most bulletin boards are free, and even those that do charge a registration fee invite users to spend some time online at no charge before paying the nominal fee. There are many bulletin boards available, and they vary widely in features and quality. Some of these systems are operated by a single user on a small PC with one phone line; others are run on powerful PCs or minicomputers that are connected to multiple lines thus allowing multiple users to access the system at the same time.

The best way to find out more about a BBS system is to call it up and request information. It is probably wise to begin with a local BBSs to avoid mounting up long distance charges. Experiment with the features that are offered and try to become a validated user so that you can have full access to all the functions. Keep in mind that some "boards" are well worth the time and money spent on them, while others are not.

Bulletin board systems, which are typically managed on small budgets by one person, come and go very quickly. One may be "up" (in operation) for a few weeks or months only to be discontinued soon after. Or one may fade from operation only to be revived later in a different form. As a result, it is difficult at any time to provide a list of bulletin boards that is completely accurate and up-to-date. However, to help you get started, we have provided a list of bulletin boards with a religious focus that are presently up and running:

Northeast

Nor'Easter	603-432-6711	Londonderry NH
Freedom Infonet	609-587-4847	Mercerville NJ

Mid Atlantic

Refuge	215-785-0895	Bristol PA
BSCCN	814-676-0407	Oil City PA
Christian Info Service	301-862-3160	California MD
Christian Resource	804-543-0830	Norfolk VA

South

The Rising Son	606-276-0132	Lexington KY
Genesis	318-352-8311	Natchitoches KY
Grace Base	901-452-0168	Memphis TN
The House of ICHTHYS	305-360-2991	Deerfield Beach FL

| The Revelation | 404-944-8059 | Atlanta GA |
| The Resistance | 502-863-2243 | Georgetown KY |

Midwest

Agape	806-795-9003	Lubbock TX
Christian Computing	816-331-4161	Belton MO
The Cuttin' Board	419-244-4597	Toledo OH
Ministry Resource Board	414-832-9177	Neenah WI
CCCBBS	618-253-3608	Harrisburg IL
SBC Info Exchange	314-636-3272	Jefferson City MO
SALT	219-262-0648	Elkhart IN

West

Believer's Board	714-457-1019	Lake Forrest CA
Logos	408-899-4552	Seaside CA
CORUNUM	714-531-2298	Fountain Valley CA
The Shepherd's Flock	714-838-4689	Irvine CA
In His Service	714-279-6987	Norco CA
Three Angels Online	619-377-5700	Ridgecrest CA

In Closing

One way to expand your religious and Bible study horizons is to enter the exhilarating world of telecommunications and online services. Armed with just a modem and communications software, you can access vast libraries of theological knowledge, receive the latest religious news, and communicate with Christians both around the corner and around the world.

An enormous storehouse of religious knowledge is available through your telephone line. Why not tap into this storehouse by investing in a modem and software? Then the next time you are puzzling over an intriguing discovery or a perplexing question, you can call a nearby bulletin board and "discuss" it with someone else!

Chapter Nine

Not for Kids Only:
Educational and Recreational Software

> ". . . a cheerful heart has a
> continual feast."
> Proverbs 15:15 (NRSV)

ould you like to go back to biblical times and relive the adventures of David and Goliath, Moses and the Exodus, Onesimus (the runaway slave of Philemon), or Noah and the ark? How about going on a treasure hunt for pieces of a mystery Bible verse, or becoming a soldier for the Lord, wearing the full armor of God?

You see, learning about the Bible does not have to be work, it can be fun! Right along with the explosion of Bible study software has come a new generation of educational and recreational Bible software. There are an amazing variety of Bible programs available for fun and learning that everyone in the family can enjoy.

In this chapter we are going to highlight Christian software for recreation and education, including children's programs, software that explores a certain period of time or events in biblical history, and programs designed to quiz on Bible facts. For those who want something special to get them through the day, we will include a Christian information manager complete with a calendar, a schedule for events, and cartoons.

The distinction between educational and recreational software is not always precise since some packages encompass elements of both. This means that there will be some overlap in the categories that follow: recreational software, children's software, and multimedia/other software. The first category examines programs that are designed for the entire family, even though the main audience will probably be children and youth. The children's software section features programs that are designed both in presentation and content specifically for children. The final section presents multimedia products and related programs. The descriptions of these products will help you determine if a specific program is right for you.

Recreational Software

The programs in the category of recreational software vary in what they offer. Some of them are arcade-type adventure games designed purely for entertainment, while others combine entertainment with education about biblical times, people, and facts. The programs in this category can be enjoyed equally by adults and children.

BIBLE ADVENTURES. Noah's Ark, David and Goliath, Moses in Egypt—these are three of the most well-known Old Testament stories, and BIBLE ADVENTURES lets you experience them all. This game package includes three video games. In "Noah's Ark" the player is challenged to gather animals and food for the ark by searching through mountains, forests, and caves. The ferocious response of the various animals increases the difficulty of this task. In the "David and Goliath" game, the player must round up the sheep and face Goliath in battle; and in the third game, "Save Baby Moses," the task is to rescue Moses from death at the hands of the Pharaoh and to outwit the soldiers in the process. These are primarily adventure arcade/video games with a biblical theme.

BIBLE BUILDER. Have you ever wanted to test your knowledge of the Bible and go on a treasure hunt at the same time? If so you will enjoy BIBLE BUILDER, a game package that is designed for the entire family.

The concept of the game is simple: Each player tries to identify a hidden Bible verse by putting together pieces of the verse script that are collected by answering questions correctly. If the player answers a question correctly, he or she receives a jigsaw puzzle piece of the verse. To win the game, the player must either identify the verse, or collect all the pieces of the puzzle before the candle burns out.

Michael, the angel, gives tips and advice, while his assistant, Gabriel, presents the puzzle pieces in response to correct answers.

BIBLE BUILDER is more than just a quiz game. It is an entertaining way to learn about the Bible, complete with full-color scenes from the Bible (including David and Goliath, the parting of the Red Sea, Noah's ark, and Daniel in the lion's den). With this program, you can become more familiar with Bible personalities and their roles in the Bible; you can learn about geography through Bible maps; you can listen to hymns; and you can look up verses in a computerized Bible.

You can also learn about Bible stories, important verses of the Bible, Holy Land geography, the Psalms, the Proverbs, the teachings of Jesus, the Parables, and much more. There are over seven hundred Bible questions, six levels of play from beginner to expert, and three modes including Old Testament, New Testament, and the complete Bible.

BIBLE CRYPTOQUOTES. This game consists of a series of cryptograms or puzzles laid out on colorful graphic backgrounds. The goal of the game is to figure out the code and discover the mystery Bible phrase or verse from the King James Version. A separate package for each of the Old and New Testaments contains in the neighborhood of five hundred different cryptograms.

COMPUTER BIBLE STORIES. This program is an excellent way to experience Bible stories with realistic depiction, narration, and sound effects. These educational Bible story programs are designed to bring to life selected stories from the Bible. Currently, "The Christmas Story," "Bible Primer," "Noah and the Ark," and "David and Goliath" are available with others in production. The educational story segments can be run at different speeds to adjust to the particular learning pace desired.

DEFENDER OF THE FAITH. An arcade/adventure game, this program explores the life and times of David from his early life to his coronation as the king of Israel. This role-playing game, which offers fast arcade-type action, has six levels of adventure, each one relating to a scene from David's life.

At level one, the player is David the Shepherd, who must face the challenge of protecting his sheep from wild animals. In the next level, "The Champion," the player attempts to defeat Goliath. As "The Musician" in level three, the player must play music in order to escape from King Saul, and as "The Hunted" in level four, the player must try to escape into the wilderness. In level five, the challenge is to obtain King Saul's water jar and spear and escape to Hachilah Hill, and in the last level the player must locate and free David's family from the dreaded fortress of Besor.

Since David was regarded as "a man after God's own heart," the player is given five hearts. When the hearts are used up, the game is over. However, if the player survives all six levels, he or she can undergo the final test in order to become a "Defender of the Faith" and the king of Israel.

For maximum enjoyment of the game it is necessary to have a high-resolution graphics card (EGA or VGA), a microprocessor of 10 MHz or greater speed, and a sound card.

EXODUS. Based on the Old Testament book of Exodus, this game has two parts: a question segment and an adventure game segment. The game starts out by asking questions based on the book of Exodus. If the player answers a question correctly the first time, he or she receives a bonus of an extra man to help in the adventure stage of the game.

In the adventure segment, the player role-plays Moses. The goal of the game is to find the manna while overcoming enemies such as soldiers and magicians, and fighting other demons such as the "weaknesses of man." As the difficulty level increases, the player must not only keep both enemies at bay but must also avoid being destroyed by falling rocks and other obstacles. The player wins by successfully navigating through a challenging sequence of fifty screens.

JOURNEY TO THE PROMISED LAND. In this entertaining educational game the player embarks on a journey to the Promised Land. Assuming the role of a Bible character, the player attempts to journey from Egypt to Canaan. Each point of progress is achieved by correctly answering a question. The program contains approximately twelve hundred questions on the Bible with varying levels of difficulty.

This game includes detailed, colorful graphics of scenes along the journey such as the mountain with the Ten Commandments, stone tablets, and lightning bolts at its summit; and Egypt with pyramids, temples, and palm trees. The objective of the game is to reach Jericho where the walls come falling down.

ONESIMUS. The life and times of Onesimus, the runaway slave of Philemon, are presented in this role-playing game. As in the biblical story, the player (as Onesimus) attempts to reach Rome in order to meet Paul and become a Christian. Trials along the way take place in deserts, forests, and rivers; there is even an attack by alligators!

Moving through thirty different levels of adventure, the player attempts to complete three tasks: (1) find the keys needed to unlock doors, (2) uncover gemstones that open up special passageways, and (3) locate apples that give extra strength.

The game offers fine VGA graphics and will produce excellent sound with a sound card.

QUEST OF THE SCROLL SCHOLAR. How good are you at identifying Bible characters? If given a few descriptive verses, can you correctly guess the character? In QUEST OF THE SCROLL SCHOLAR the player must search through ancient scrolls to come up with clues to the identities of dozens of biblical characters. The scrolls contain hundreds of clues including Scripture references. The game features adventure-action sequences and Bible questions.

The program offers various modes of play, including Whiz Kid, Quiz Kid, and Game Buster. It has both high-resolution VGA graphics and sound effects capabilities.

SPIRITUAL WARFARE. If you have ever wanted to be a soldier in the army of the Lord and wear the full armor of God, here's your chance. This video/quiz game combines pure entertainment with education. Through the exploration of a city, the player attempts to collect parts of the full armor of God. Villainous characters and other challenges designed as tests of faith try to impede the way. By answering strategic questions correctly, however, the player strengthens his or her spirit and moves on through the game. The twelve different parts to the city are developed with high quality color graphics and include gospel music as a background.

Children's Software

A renewed interest in recreational Bible programs has brought about a number of exciting and engaging Bible programs for children.

Many of these programs use the latest techniques in graphics and sound technologies to help them come alive.

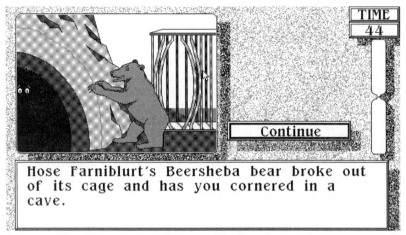

Fig. 9.1 A Bible adventure game. (Courtesy of NavPress.)

WHERE IN THE WORLD IS AMAZ'N BLAZ'N? This game centers on the adventures of the Old Testament character, Joseph, who had a coat of many colors. However, in this game Joseph has a colt of many colors, which acts like the mascot of the game cheering the player on through each step.

Four separate games comprise AMAZ'N BLAZ'N. The first game has four adventures from the life of Joseph, including "Pit to Pinnacle" (Genesis 41), "Down Under" (Genesis 39), "Dreams and Screams" (Genesis 37), and "Jail Jolt" (Genesis 41). Each adventure segment has a spiritual value lesson and includes traveling through Old Testament places, finding items, overcoming obstacles, and meeting with different characters along the way.

Another game, "Coloring Book," provides cartoons to color, and the "Puzzle Game" is a jigsaw-puzzle of cartoon characters that must be fit back together using a keyboard or mouse.

The "Honey Word" section of the program presents Emmett Cooper's Honey Word system to teach the books of the Bible using memory techniques such as pairing sounds. Thus Titus is paired with tortoise, and the image of a turtle appears on the screen.

While these games are designed primarily for children ages five to ten, some parts of the program, particularly the adventures of Joseph, are best played by children with the help of an adult.

BIBLE PAINT AND LEARN. The goal of this program is to let children enjoy coloring Bible pictures that encourage them to think about biblical times and people. Each picture is accompanied by a story and an animated, musical quiz. After painting the picture the child can turn it into a jigsaw puzzle.

Some of the other features of the program include sound effects that play while the child fills in the pictures and symbolic icons to help the child learn the system. In this program kids have fun painting and coloring while they listen to Bible stories and thus improve their knowledge of Bible facts and people. The program is designed for children ages three and up.

BIBLE TIME FUN. While this set of games is designed for children, it can be entertaining for the entire family. There are two separate packages, Old and New Testament, and each one has a wide selection of games. There are no less than five different games in each software package, including "Bible Stories," "Bible Time Paint," "Bible Time Fun," "Bible Puzzles," "Verse Search," and "Concentration."

The "Bible Stories" section presents a paraphrased Bible story (such as one about Noah) as the basis for other activities such as learning facts, putting a puzzle together, doing word scrambles, and playing a maze/verse search game.

"Bible Time Paint" is a creative program that presents a color picture from which the colors can be deleted and colored in by hand. It includes a color-cycle effect that lets children move the colors around, and they can also create their own pictures and diagrams.

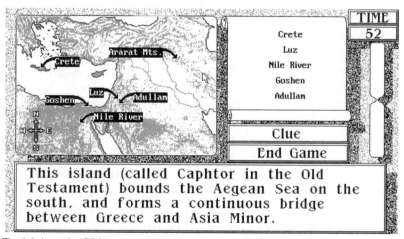

Fig. 9.2 Learning Bible geography on the computer. (Courtesy of NavPress.)

Multimedia and
Other Christian Software

Although many of the games already discussed offer multi-media elements, the multimedia games mentioned in this section go farther in integrating graphics, sound, video, and text to produce recreational and educational activities that are more advanced than most existing computer software programs.

The other programs in this section (GUIDED PRAYER JOURNAL, IN HIS TIME, HEARTWARMERS) are included because of the unique resources they offer.

Multimedia Products

GERASENE DEMONIAC. The Bible is a dynamic book of history, people, and events that shaped our world. While many biblical programs have attempted to capture these elements, an innovative approach beyond ordinary software is the GERASENE DEMONIAC, a multimedia journey into the biblical story of Mark 5:1–20.

This program lets the user experience the film "Out of the Tombs"; compare versions of Bible texts and how they were translated from the original Greek; see the story in rap and chant styles; watch teens responding to the story; keep a journal of personal thoughts; view video segments on the history and geography of the area; and create slide shows.

The program is designed for a teen and young adult audience. It uses the latest in multimedia technology and requires not only a personal computer but video and sound cards, external speakers, and a laserdisc player. While the hardware requirements are higher, this innovative program allows the player to experience the Bible in a totally new way.

The program is produced by the American Bible Society, and a second program in the series is planned on "The Prodigal Son."

MULTIMEDIA FAMILY BIBLE allows users not only to read Bible texts but also to see and hear what they are reading about! Designed to be used by all members of the family, it provides the King James Version text together with the ability to search for words and phrases. Bible verses can be compared in separate windows and can also be put in a word processor file or printed out directly.

The most exciting parts of the program are its multimedia features that include fabulous reproductions of biblical paintings, such as Jesus and his disciples at the Last Supper. The user can be with Noah as he builds the ark, can walk with Jesus to Emmaus, or be on the scene when Daniel is thrust into the lion's den.

And that's not all—while these multimedia features are presented a Biblical narrative describes what is happening against a background of music. The user can choose a feature presentation of the great stories of the Bible, multimedia presentations of stories from both the Old and New Testaments, or by selecting a passage in Scripture can have that particular story brought to life.

The system was created for children as well as adults and is easy to use. As an added bonus this program does not require a CD-ROM drive.

Other Bible Programs

GUIDED PRAYER JOURNAL enables the user to schedule, organize, and view personal prayer requests. Through a selection of pull-down menus, the user sets up a system to display each day's prayer requests. It is possible to view the list in different ways and to print out the requests in various formats. It is also possible to add requests, change requests, and use the Scheduler to schedule the presentation of requests.

HEARTWARMERS FOR WINDOWS is a Microsoft-Windows based program that displays inspirational and motivational thoughts each day of the year. The program includes Bible verses as well as quotations from notables such as Abraham Lincoln and Mother Theresa. The user can search the thoughts, verses, and quotations by topic, author, and key words; use the built-in calendar; and also print out the thoughts and quotes. The program requires Microsoft Windows to run.

IN HIS TIME, an information manager with a Christian theme, is designed to help the user organize events at home and work. Running under Microsoft Windows, the program provides a friendly, graphical approach to managing time and activities. The program offers a number of different features, including a "Things to Do" reminder list, appointment schedules, a special "Events to Remember" facility, a personal prayer diary designed to record prayer requests (and answers), as well as daily Scripture verses and Christian cartoons. It also provides an electronic address book and a Bible reading schedule. Colorful icons guide the user through the program and serve as reminders of upcoming appointments. All of this information can be printed out in a personalized calendar.

Fig. 9.3 Personal calendar. (Courtesy of Colonnade.)

In Closing

If you are looking for an entertaining way for both you and your family to learn about the Bible, these computer Bible games can be a help. While the games vary in how much education they provide as opposed to entertainment, many of the products in this new generation of Bible-oriented games make it possible to experience the lives and times of people in the Bible in a new and exciting format.

You can go on a treasure hunt for clues about mystery Bible verses while you test your knowledge of Bible facts; take on the role of Moses during the Exodus or David as he becomes King of Israel; be Onesimus, the slave who runs away to Rome and becomes a Christian; experience the events of the Gerasene demoniac through a combination of sound, video, and graphics that will make you think you are actually there. Bible games are not just fun—they are learning experiences too!

PART III

Applying Computer Technology to Bible Study

Chapter Ten

Biblical Bytes:
Methods of Computer Bible Study

"Study to show thyself approved
unto God."
2 Timothy 2:15 (KJV)

Where would we be without pieces and parts? They let us take things apart and figure them out and put them back together again . . . like the parts of a computer that we have talked about. But what about the parts of a book—like the Bible? If we want to understand the Bible, a good place to begin is by considering and analyzing one of its basic parts—*words*. As we understand the individual words in their contexts, we can better understand the Bible as a whole—its concepts, doctrines, themes, and truths; its people, places, and times; its verses, chapters, books, and Testaments.

Computers are particularly helpful in Bible study because they generate lists of information that save us time and effort. But what do we do with the lists of information? This is where methods of Bible study can help. Computers generate, as it were, the pieces of the puzzle, and Bible study methods help us put the pieces together so we can see the overall picture. So in the next few chapters we will focus on how to do computer Bible studies based on:

(a) a simple unit of communication—the **word**

(b) a simple computer function—the **word search**.

With these basic tools we will explore the following methods of Bible study:

- **word study**
- **biographical study**
- **historical-geographical study**
- **topical study**

There are two basic principles of Bible interpretation that highlight the purpose for these methods of Bible study. First, we must always remember that the Bible was originally written to someone else who lived a long time ago in another part of the world where they spoke a different language. Therefore, to understand the Bible clearly, we need to study each passage from the perspective of the original writers and readers. Only then can we properly appreciate its meaning and determine its significance for our lives today.

In this regard, the word study method will relate to the fact that the original writer and audience spoke a different language than we speak; the biographical study method will relate to the fact that they lived in different circumstances in a unique culture; and the historical-geographical study method will consider their different part of the world and time in history.

A second principle of Bible interpretation is that on most subjects, God's truth is not communicated completely in any one passage. Therefore, to correctly comprehend that truth we need to study what the Bible teaches on a given subject in different parts of the Bible—we need to consider the whole counsel of God on any given subject or theme. Thus, the chapter on the topical method of study will demonstrate how to study a topic from the broad perspective of the entire Bible.

Word Studies Are for Everyone

The process of researching and studying a Bible word is simple, yet extremely gratifying; it opens up endless avenues of information and insight. However, many people are intimidated by the thought of studying Bible words because they believe, erroneously, that this requires a thorough knowledge of the original biblical languages—either Hebrew, Greek, or Aramaic. A typical initial response is, "But I don't know any Greek or Hebrew. I couldn't possibly study Bible words!"

In reality, nothing could be further from the truth. With the abundant Bible-study tools and resources available today, it is not necessary to have a specialized knowledge of Greek or Hebrew to do word studies. In fact, with the capabilities of advanced computerized programs and study aids, it is possible to study Bible words without researching dozens of reference books or even opening a printed Bible!

For those who have limited experience in Bible study or biblical languages, the purpose of the next few chapters will be to demonstrate how to complete accurate word studies using electronic Bibles and other study tools, and how to apply this process to a variety of Bible study methods. For pastors, seminary students, and others with previous experience in various methods of Bible study, these next few chapters will demonstrate how the computer can make the study process more precise and efficient.

Computer Bible Study—Enjoyable and Effective

The computer Bible study methods we present in the following chapters have been developed to allow you to study the Bible on your computer effectively and to enjoy doing it! We do not want you to feel like Christopher Columbus, who, according to J. M. Braude, did not know where he was going when he started, did not know where he was when he got there, and when he got back, did not know where he had been! That is why we suggest Bible study methods that (1) are systematic, (2) limit the scope of study, and (3) increase understanding through personal interaction questions.

Systematic Study

The Bible studies in the following chapters provide a *systematic* method of study. It goes without saying that you will gain

much more information for the time spent if you study systemati-
cally rather than haphazardly. The system of study we will outline
below is somewhat like the work of a scientist who

> questions and explores
>   gathers data
>   correlates the data
>   makes observations and draws conclusions
>   determines how these observations affect life.

Thus, in our process of computer Bible study we will:

explore	search for a word or a string of words
collect	keep notes of data either in a notebook or in a computer file
organize	arrange data in charts, graphs, etc.
consider	draw conclusions from the data (ask questions!!)
apply	act on what we discover

Each of these steps will be applied to four separate methods of Bible
study.

Boundaries in Bible Study

The process of Bible study we suggest will help you to establish *limits* to the scope of your study and will help you to define a
direction to that study. Anyone who attempts to tackle massive
amounts of data without a determined boundary more often than
not ends up feeling frustrated and confused.

For example, consider what would happen if you sat down
at the computer and decided to study the biblical concept of "love"
without setting any parameters for the study. A fairly routine search
of the word *love* throughout your entire electronic Bible would
produce hundreds of occurrences of the word in its various grammatical forms.   But what do you do with literally hundreds of
listings of *love* with multiple nuances of meaning and application?
You would probably feel overwhelmed and without a sense of
direction for the use of the data, very likely, would not make optimum use of the information gathered.

It would be much more beneficial, and much less frustrating, to limit the scope of such a study to a particular method—a word study or perhaps a theme study—within a restricted boundary: a chapter or a book. A good starting point might be to study the development of the theme of love in I Corinthians 13 and compare those findings to other passages that use the same biblical words and concepts. Even this carefully defined study would provide material for hours of research. However, by limiting the scope of the study and determining the direction or system of study, you would be limiting the amount of data to process and would know exactly how you wanted to process the information you gathered. In short, the study would be much more profitable and enjoyable!

Ask Questions

Someone has said, "The inquisitive mind is the acquiring mind." That is why one of the basic tools of Bible study is asking *questions.* We have found that a key to understanding a Bible text (or word, or verse, or chapter) is to ask questions of that text. So you will find that each chapter includes a list of questions created specifically for the computer Bible study method explained in that chapter. We also suggest questions to ask in each application section.

The questions we list are not intended to be used in making new, outstanding discoveries. Rather, we simply want to encourage each reader to look for what the Bible has been saying for centuries and to apply that message personally. We encourage you to:

- ask questions to make observations
- ask questions to interpret your observations

The Five Steps of Computer Bible Study

Step one — Explore

The initial step in the Bible-study methods we outline is to *explore.* This involves searching through an electronic Bible for data that is pertinent to each particular study. For the most part, this will involve searching for a word, or a string of words, and comparing passages both within a translation and (when accessible) across multiple translations. Depending upon the subject presented in each chapter, you will want to search the Bible text for a particular word or string of words that represent a theme or topic, a doctrine, the name of a person or a place, or perhaps an event. This will be explained in detail in each chapter.

Step two — Collect Data

The second step is to collect the data. The process for collecting data that we have found most rewarding is to use information from the text or passage that is being searched to answer questions that are pertinent to the emphasis of that study, For example, when we perform a word search for a topical study we will ask a set of questions that are relevant to Bible topics. If we are working through a historical study, we will ask a set of questions that relate to Bible history.

The information you gather by finding the answers to these questions will be necessary to complete the study process, so you will want to keep a record of your findings. This can be done either by writing your observations in a note pad or by saving the information you find to a computer file or electronic notepad where it will be stored until you want to print it out. Most computerized Bibles are programmed to print verses in a few seconds with a simple keystroke or at the touch of a mouse. At this stage you will simply want to record all of your findings as you discover them. Do not worry about organizing the material—that is the next step.

Step three — Organize the Data

As you search for words and gather answers to strategic questions you will want to take notes and write down the information you gather. However, to make this information useful it needs to be analyzed, summarized, and organized in manageable portions. There are myriad ways to organize data, but among the most helpful are charts, graphs, and outlines. The secret to developing a useful chart or graph is to classify the data by categorical distinctions and arrange the classified material in a defined area—a column, a box, a line, etc. Classifying the data involves discovering what different aspects of the subject are discussed in the collected data, labeling these aspects, and grouping together all the verses on each different phase of the subject. When you are sorting through data on the computer, it is helpful to give labels to groupings, then you can find them or sort them by their labels either automatically or by the "move" feature.

Remember, the keys to making serviceable charts or graphs or outlines are: *simplicity* and *brevity*. When you want to organize your data keep these things in mind:

1. Arrange the basic ideas to be seen at a glance.

2. Use small, manageable amounts of information.

3. Compress the information into words and phrases.

4. Present your own observations.

Charts and graphs like those we have included in the following chapters can be created quickly and quite effortlessly with computer programs that have window capabilities. Once you begin developing your own charts and graphs you will discover endless possibilities for organizing and presenting your findings.

Step four — Consider the Graphs and Charts and Draw Conclusions

Charts, graphs, and outlines are a vital step in the process of computer Bible study, but they are not the ultimate goal, because even organized data is only useful to us as it applies to everyday life. This is particularly true of the Bible, which was given to us precisely for the purpose of affecting our lives. So all the data we can gather is only meaningful as we interpret it—that is as we explain the meaning of our findings in relationship to daily living.

When we draw conclusions from the data, we are looking for (1) broad, universal spiritual truths, (2) biblical doctrines, (3) commands, (4) precepts, (5) principles, and (6) promises that are applicable across the spectrum of believers, and to the Church across the centuries.

One of the most productive ways of drawing spiritual conclusions is to ask questions that identify and personalize the truths discovered in the organized data. The goal should be: *to discover general principles or truths that are applicable to audiences across time and space.* We need to be aware that some passages of Scripture are applicable specifically to the original audience in the period of history when they were written. Our goal is to find cross-cultural principles for today. Thus, as part of step four in each chapter, we will suggest questions to help identify these principles. Use these questions as a springboard to create additional questions of your own.

Step five — Apply the Principles to Daily Life

This is where the process of taking account and actualizing our findings takes place. It is answering not only the question

What does this mean to me?

but also the question,

What should I do about it?

In determining our response we need to keep in mind two dimensions: (1) our relationship with God, and (2) our relationship with others. This step transfers the spiritual truths and principles into the realm of the practical world where they can make a difference—in our lives and through our lives to those around us. Rick Warren, in his book *Dynamic Bible Study Methods* (Wheaton: Victor Books, 1973) suggests that application be:

personal

practical

possible

measurable

In this step we will look at the principles we discovered in step four and determine what our responsibility is with regard to those principles. Bible study is not complete until it has affected our lives, which in turn should affect the world around us.

In Closing

Each of the next four chapters presents a distinct method of computer Bible study that incorporates the five steps outlined above. To help you understand the distinctives of these methods of Bible study, each chapter will include a sample study based on the book of Philippians.

As you progress through these chapters, we are convinced that you will be amazed and enthusiastic about the speed and efficiency of computer Bible study. We are also certain that you will enjoy the excitement of discovery that only comes from personal research and study. It is our hope that this excitement will result in personal and practical application of the truths you learn. We want it to impact your life—and the world through your life.

Chapter Eleven

Working with Words:
Computer Word Study

> *"The Lord's words are pure, like silver*
> *purified by fire, like silver purified*
> *seven times over."*
> *Psalm 12:6 (NCV)*

ords, the basic units of thought in the Bible, are a good place to begin computer Bible study. Over six thousand words comprise today's English translations, but that figure is easily dwarfed by the original versions of Hebrew, Greek, or Aramaic that, together, have almost twice as many words—well over eleven thousand. Since it is important not to study the English words apart from their corresponding original words, that means we have more than seventeen thousand words to work with in our study—a thought that is almost as exciting as it is daunting!

Performing a Word Study

Explore

The first question that probably comes to your mind is "which word should I study?" You can choose to study any word that piques your interest. It may be a subject you have puzzled about for some time, or it may be a topic that is particularly relevant to your life situation—like *patience* or *love* or *understanding* around report card time. Another option is to choose a word that is significant to a particular passage or book of the Bible.

In this instance, to determine what word or words are significant, read through a passage, chapter, or entire book. Notice:

1. words that are repeated frequently,

2. words that convey crucial (key) ideas,

3. words that are used as symbols, and

4. words that express comparisons in similes or metaphors.

Make a note of these words either on a piece of paper or in a computer file. This process allows you to define the parameters of your study. Once you have determined a list of key words, narrow the list to one or two words or concepts and choose which one you want to study.

Collect

Once you have chosen a word to study, the first step in understanding the use of that word in the Bible is to determine the *meaning* of the word. Keep in mind that when we study the Bible we must consistently take care to understand that meaning in the context of the Bible. In other words, we cannot determine the meaning of a word based on what we think it means or what it might mean to us today. We must determine the meaning of a word based on:

• What it meant to the author.

• What it meant to the readership-audience.

• What it means in its particular biblical context.

1. **Consult a Bible dictionary and concordance**. How do we determine the meaning of a word? A dictionary is a good place to start—that is, a Bible dictionary. We want to find the definition of the word, and while an English dictionary would be sufficient in many circumstances, we must take a different course of action

when we are working with biblical words—we must discover the meaning of the original language word that was used by the biblical writer. So although an English dictionary would be helpful in determining the general nuances of the English word that is used in the Bible, it must be supplemented by discovering the meaning of the original biblical word, because the words from our language that are used to translate biblical words may not convey precisely the same idea as the biblical word did.

At this point you may be thinking, "Then I do need to know Greek and Hebrew after all!" No, all you need is a concordance and a Bible dictionary that gives the range of meaning of each English word and suggests which meaning best fits the specific passage you are studying. To find the right word in a Bible dictionary, start by looking up the word you want to study in a concordance. The concordance will list not only the passages where the word occurs but will also identify the Hebrew, Aramaic, or Greek word that is used in the original language. This will be accompanied by a number that directs you to a special index that provides the biblical word in English. Once you have found this specific English word, you will want to look up the meaning of that word and find the definition given for it in a Bible dictionary.

As you continue your studies of this word, always study the concordance list of Hebrew and Greek words first, rather than the English word, because when you study with just the English word it is too easy to mix underlying Greek and Hebrew words that are translated by the one English word. You do not want to end up mixing apples and oranges or even mixing Jonathan apples, Delicious apples, McIntosh apples, etc. *The meaning of the original biblical word always determines the meaning of the English word, not vice versa.* For example, the English word *another* has a distinct meaning in Galations 1:6 and 7 depending on the Greek word that was used originally. In verse six the Greek word actually means "of a different kind," while in verse seven the Greek word means "another of the same kind." Although both are translated *another,* each actually conveys a very different meaning in the original language. And that is the meaning we want to work with.

If your computer does not print by Greek or Hebrew words or numbers, then study together the passages listed in a concordance that have the same Greek word number. Make a printout of these references and mark with a colored marker all references to the same number. Then you will be sure to study all the references of the same Greek or Hebrew word.

Many Bible dictionaries and concordances are included as part of the Bible software packages that are available today, or they can be purchased separately as add-ons. Here is a list of those that are most widely used:

Strong, J. *Exhaustive Concordance of the Bible*, Abingdon, 1980.

Vine, W. E., M. F. Unger, and W. White. *An Expository Dictionary of Biblical Words*, Nelson, 1984.

Kittel, G. and G. Friedrich, eds. *Theological Dictionary of the New Testament*, Eerdmans, 1985.

Harris, R. L. et al., eds. *Theological Wordbook of the Old Testament*, Moody, 1980.

Van Gemeren, W. et al., eds. *New International Dictionary of Old Testament Theology*, Zondervan, 1975.

Brown, C., ed. *New International Dictionary of New Testament Theology*, Zondervan, 1975.

The concordance and dictionary not only list the occurrences of a biblical word, they also give a precise definition. Sometimes the etymology of the word will be noted. (This refers to the root word in the original Greek, Hebrew, or Aramaic that this word came from or the meaning of two words that were combined to make a new compound word.) Be sure to record in your notebook the definition and additional information you gather about the meaning of the word.

2. **Compare translations**. Another source of insight into the meaning of a word is a comparative analysis of various translations of the Bible. If you have access to several translations (either printed or computerized) compare specific passages and verses and write down how different translators used the word or how they translated the original word in the same passage possibly using a different (though similar) English word. One translator may use a single word to convey the idea of the original Greek or Hebrew word while another translator may use a phrase. One translator may use one word to convey the same idea throughout a passage or book while another translator may use various words.

Take note of these variations and record them in your notebook. By reflecting on the different ways to express the same idea in English, you will gain insight into a word's meaning.

3. **Verify How the Author Is Using the Word**. To fully understand a word or phrase you will need to discover how it is used

- in other passages of a book,
- in other books by the same author,
- in other parts of the testament, and
- throughout the entire Bible.

This information can be quickly gathered by doing a word search through a defined area of text. Observe how the author uses the word in other parts of the book and how he uses it in other books he has written. In every search, always focus on the original biblical word, not just the English word. Then note how other authors use the word in the same testament. Do they use the word in different ways? How does this affect its meaning in various contexts? As a result of this study you will want to list how the word is used most frequently, primarily by the author but also by other authors throughout the Scriptures. It would also be helpful to copy instances when an author *defines* the word either with a straightforward description or by means of an illustration or an example from life.

Use the following questions as a guide to help you collect data that will explain the meaning of the word you are studying.

Questions for a Word Study:

1. How often does this word occur?

2. What do I understand to be the meaning of this word?

3. In what way does the meaning of the biblical word used by the author agree with and differ from our normal use of the English word used to translate it?

4. Does the author use the word in various ways, or with various meanings? What kind of context fits each of these different meanings?

5. Does the author define or explain the word? Is an illustration given or a comparison (metaphor or simile)?

6. Does the author use the word in other writings? Is the meaning similar in other occurrences? Different?

7. Do other authors use the word in their writings? Is the meaning similar or different?

 Organize

At this point you will need to trim the total amount of data down to a workable size. This means you will want to classify and group the material in categories. You will need to summarize your findings and select a system for presenting the data. This may be a graph, a chart, perhaps a diagram, or a table. Initially it will probably be most helpful to devise simple charts of basic categories. From there you can branch out into more complicated graphs and diagrams.

 Consider

One of the most helpful ways of drawing conclusions from the organized data is to answer questions. Here are some questions that will help you to distinguish themes, principles, doctrines, and precepts from the information gathered in a word study.

1. What key ideas are emphasized? What general principles express these ideas?

2. What things are believers encouraged or commanded to do?

3. How can I respond to the truths I have found?

4. Are there promises to claim?

5. Are there truths to believe?

6. Is there sin to avoid, confess, or forsake?

7. Is there an example to follow?

8. Is there a command to obey?

 Apply

Once you have distinguished general truths and principles, you will want to decide how they should affect your life. It is not enough to understand what God's Word says, we must decide what it says to us!

A Word Study in Philippians

Exploring and Collecting the Data

As we read through the book of Philippians several times we made a list of words that Paul used frequently throughout the book or that seemed to indicate key ideas for him. From that list we chose to do a word study on *rejoice*. To determine the meaning of this word we answered the following questions by performing word searches of the verb *rejoice* (*chairō*) and a noun, *joy* (*chara*). Then we answered the questions suggested for a word study.

1. How often does the word *rejoice* occur?

A search of the word *rejoice* and its derivatives based on a Greek word indicated that it appears twelve times in the book of Philippians. A second word search indicated that the word *joy* occurs six times. Since there are only four chapters in the book, eighteen times is a fairly frequent use of the verb and noun forms of the word *rejoice*. It would appear to be a key concept for Paul in this book.

Ref.	English	Strong's number	Greek	Concordance Definition
1:18	rejoice	5463	*chairō* (verb)	to be calmly happy (2x)
1:26	rejoicing	2745	*kauchēma*	the act of boasting
2:16	rejoice	2745	*kauchēma*	" "
2:17	rejoice	4796	*sugchairō* (verb)	to congratulate
2:18	rejoice	4796	*sugchairō* (verb)	" "
2:28	rejoice	5463	*chairō* (verb)	to be calmly happy
3:1	rejoice	5463	*chairō* (verb)	" "
3:3	rejoice	2744	*kauchaŏmai* (verb)	to boast, glory
4:4	rejoice	5463	*chairō* (verb)	to be calmly happy
4:4	rejoice	5463	*chairō* (verb)	" "
4:10	rejoiced	5463	*chairō* (verb)	" "
1:4	joy	5479	*chara* (noun)	great gladness
1:25	joy	5479	"	" "
2:2	joy	5479	"	" "

2:17	joy	5463	*chairō* (verb)	to be calmly happy
2:18	joy	5463	"	" "
4:1	joy	5479	*chara* (noun)	great gladness

2. What do I understand to be the meaning of the word *rejoice?*

A basic English dictionary definition of *rejoice* is "to feel joy or great delight." It would probably include the concept of being happy and content, possibly including outward indications by a smile, a laugh, and perhaps a song.

3. Does Paul use the word *rejoice* with the meaning I understand or with a different meaning?

As we discovered in our word search and concordance search, the English word *rejoice* was translated from several original Greek words, each of which has a slightly different definition. (Note the differences on the chart above.) We looked for the Greek words in a Bible dictionary and found some further information:

chairō - is the word for joy that is used most often in the New Testament. It refers to both a state of joy and to the things that bring joy. The meaning is to rejoice, be glad, be joyful, or to have joy. The form *sugchairō* means to rejoice together with someone.

chara - is a noun form meaning joy.

kauchēma/kauchaòmai - while these words were translated by the same English word *rejoice,* their meaning is slightly different in Greek: to boast (in a good or bad sense), or to glory in something. They are actually synonymns of *chairō.*

To avoid misunderstandings, we chose to limit the remainder of our word study to the Greek words *chairō* and *chara;* we eliminated *kauchēma/kaucheòmai* from this phase of our study.

4. Does Paul use the word *rejoice* (*chairō/chara*) in various ways, or with various meanings?

Depending on the context of the surrounding words or verses, the word has a different shade of meaning although the basic concept is the same. This was particularly obvious when we compared the occurrences of *rejoice* (*chairō*/*chara*) in several translations. For example:

1:18 - being **happy** when Christ is preached (Phillips)

2:17 - to be **glad** and to share that **gladness** (NEB)

2:18 - wanting others to be **happy** (Living Bible)

2:28 - being **thankful** when Epaphroditus arrives (Living Bible)

4:4 - be full of **joy** always (Living Bible)

4:10 - Paul was **grateful** that the Philippians were helping him again (Living Bible)

As we looked more carefully at the context surrounding each occurrence of the word *rejoice* we found that Paul defined the concept of joy through four different situations.

1. Paul rejoices because of encouraging circumstances:

   a. A financial gift 1:5; 4:10

   b. Hope for release from jail 2:25

   c. Epaphroditus recovers from illness and plans to return home 2:27–29

2. Paul rejoices because of the spiritual health of his converts at Philippi:

   a. Saints are living in harmony 2:2

   b. Philippians themselves are fellow believers 4:1

3. Paul rejoices because of his effective witness for Christ in spite of adversity:

   a. Christ preached even though from improper motives 1:18, 19 (used twice for emphasis)

   b. Even martyrdom will bring glory to Christ 2:17 (used twice for emphasis)

   c. Philippians should rejoice if Paul's life is taken in missionary endeavor 2:18 (used twice for emphasis)

4. Paul rejoices because of his relationship with the Lord 3:1, 4:4 (twice).

5. Does Paul define or explain the word *rejoice?* Does he give an illustration of its meaning or make comparisons?

Paul does not give a definition of the word *rejoice,* but he includes an illustration from his life that enhances our understanding of the term. That is, in spite of the fact that he was in prison and could not move about freely to preach, and those who could preach without hindrance were doing so out of vanity and self-interest, Paul was still happy—because both in his circumstances and in spite of strife, the gospel was going forth.

6. Does Paul use the word *rejoice* in his other writings? Is the meaning in those other instances similar to his use in Philippians or different?

By increasing the boundaries of our word search to include other books written by Paul, we found that he used this form of the original Greek word (*chairō/chara*) for *rejoice* frequently in his writings. Here are just a few of the many examples we found:

Rom. 12:12	rejoice	*chairō*
1 Cor. 12:26	rejoicing together	"
Col. 1:24	rejoice	"
1 Thess. 5:16	rejoice	"

7. Do other writers use the word *rejoice* (*chairō/chara*) in their writings? Do they use it with a similar meaning or different?

This time we increased the boundaries of our word search to include the entire New Testament. We found that several writers used the word for *rejoicing* (*chairō*) in the same way as Paul did. For example:

Matthew - Matt. 2:10

Luke - Luke 1:14, 13:17, and Acts 5:41, 8:39

John - John 3:29, 14:28, 2 John 4, 3 John 3

Peter - 1 Pet. 4:13

Organizing the Data

There are any number of ways we could have organized the data we collected from our word search through the book of Philippians, but we decided upon three that were simple and helpful for our purposes.

A. In the first chart we listed the verses where the words *rejoice* or *joy* occurred in chronological sequence to determine if there was a development of a theme through this arrangement. You can see the various nuances of the theme of *rejoicing* that we observed.

B. In the second chart we organized each situation when Paul used the word *rejoice* according to three questions: Who? What? Why? Based on the chart we then developed a wheel graph indicating the reasons for rejoicing.

C. In the third chart we arranged various translations of key Scriptures for comparison (only a portion appears here).

Philippians Theme: Rejoicing	Reasons for Rejoicing
1:4 making request with *joy*	**Rejoicing** because the gospel goes forth
1:18 rejoicing in the progress of the gospel	
1:25 *joy* of faith	**Rejoicing** in Christian partnership
2:2 fulfill my *joy*	
2:17 *rejoices* in being poured out	**Rejoicing** in sacrifice and service
2:18 they should *rejoice* and be glad also	
2:28 they will *rejoice*	
3:1 *rejoice* in the Lord	**Rejoicing** in the provision of Christ
4:1 Believers are Paul's *joy*	**Rejoicing** through Christian fellowship
4:4 *Rejoice* always	**Rejoicing** through correct thoughts
4:10 Paul *rejoiced* at their care	**Rejoicing** through Christian love and concern

WHO?	WHAT?	WHY?
Paul	**rejoiced**	in progress of gospel
Philippians	**rejoicing**	when Paul comes again
Paul	**will rejoice**	that his labors have not been in vain
Paul	**rejoices**	that he is being poured out in service
Philippians	**can rejoice**	that Paul is being poured out in service
Philippians	**rejoice**	in the Lord
Philippians	**rejoice**	in what Christ has provided in salvation
Philippians	**rejoice**	by not being anxious and by thinking "correct" thoughts
Paul	**rejoices**	that the Philippians are concerned and caring for him once again

Reasons for Rejoicing

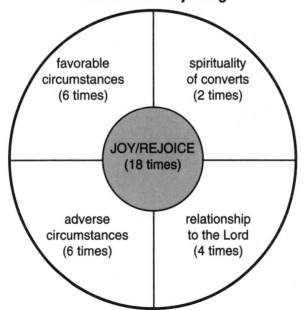

Translation Comparison of Philippians 1:18			
KJV	**RSV**	**Phillips**	**NIV**
What then?	What then?	But what does it matter?	But what does it matter?
notwithstanding every way whether in pretense or in truth	Only that in every way, whether in pretense or in truth,	However they may look at it, the fact remains (whether sincerely or not)	The important thing is that in every way, whether from false motives or true,
Christ is preached	Christ is proclaimed	Christ is being preached	Christ is preached
and I therein do **rejoice**, yea, and will **rejoice**	and in that I **rejoice**.	and that fact makes me very **happy**.	And because of this I **rejoice**.

 Considering the Data

With the three charts we were able to summarize the data and obtain: (a) an understanding of the meaning of *rejoice;* (b) an overview of some basic biblical principles. To help us in this process we answered the questions to consider from page 139. Some of our answers are listed below.

1. Experiencing joy and rejoicing should be a part of the Christian life.

2. Believers are encouraged to rejoice in the efforts of others for the Kingdom of God.

3. The gospel will be spread in spite of difficult circumstances.

4. Adversity does not overcome the sense of well being Christians experience when they have cause to rejoice.

5. A controlled thought life is necessary to maintain joy. Not

only should we avoid anxious thoughts, but we should think thoughts that are pure, truthful, and of a good report.

Making Application

When we applied the answers to these questions to our personal circumstances, we arrived at some interesting conclusions. For example:

1. We can be joyful just realizing what Christ has done for us.

2. Although we miss friends who are working as missionaries overseas, we should be happy about the work they are doing for the Lord.

3. Perhaps we need to find out more about what other believers are doing for the Kingdom of God and encourage them in their work.

4. Like Paul, we need to rejoice in spite of difficult circumstances. We also need to look beyond our short-term interests to the long-term good of the Kingdom of God. Any sacrifices we make to further the Gospel should be cause for rejoicing!

Where to Go from Here

We have just scratched the surface of possible word studies in the book of Philippians. Some other key words you might want to study are:

praise	prayer
fellowship	gospel
love	suffering
salvation	faith

or you might want to consider the phrase "in Christ."

Chapter Twelve

Bible Biographies:
Computer Biographical Study

> *"Wise people's lives get better and better."*
> *Proverbs 15:24 (NCV)*

T here are over three thousand individuals mentioned in the Bible. Some are known by one name, others like Peter are known by as many as four (Peter, Simeon, Simon, and Cephas). Over the course of their lives, some of these individuals had their names changed, like Abram, who was renamed Abraham, or Saul, who later became known as Paul. And then there are others who are not identified by name at all, such as the Samaritan woman or the man by the pool of Bethesda. But whether we know them by one name, or two, or several, all of the persons referred to in the Bible are there for a purpose and for our benefit. Through their lives we can be challenged and guided in our Christian walk. We can learn to follow their examples when they inspire us, and we can learn to avoid their mistakes when they disappoint us.

Performing a Biographical Study

Explore

Have you ever wondered how the disciples' involvement with Christ affected their families? A biographical study on the life of Peter would probably satisfy your curiosity. Or has a certain event in a Bible character's life puzzled you? For example, have you ever wondered why Ruth, a devout and highly respected young widow, slept all night at the feet of an unmarried man? These questions, and many more, can be answered by studying Bible biographies (*bio*-life, *graphy*-writing).

When we study a person's life we want to gather information about that person as a unique individual. We want to learn about his or her background, family, physical characteristics, personality, character traits, attitudes. We also want to record his or her life experiences, activities, ministry, and responses to determine the effect or significance of these factors on that individual's life as well as on the lives of others. This involves setting out events in the order of an individual's experience and then evaluating those events in terms of effects or results.

You may choose to study a Bible character because you are curious about his or her life or because that person is mentioned in a book of the Bible you are studying. The character may be someone you admire, or someone you simply cannot understand. Actually, one of the most popular reasons for doing a biographical study is to learn about the life of a Bible author as a means of understanding his writings.

Once you have decided who you want to study, you will want to search for every verse where that person is mentioned. You can do this by completing a word search for the person's name, but do not limit yourself to a word search as there are many passages that give information about an individual—Paul for example—that do not mention his name. Therefore, in this study more than in any other, it may be necessary initially to find references simply by reading a relevant text or book of the Bible and writing down or copying into a computer file every verse that mentions the person, his or her family, friends, background, etc.

These references in turn will provide names of people, places, events, etc., that can be researched through further word searches and cross-references.

When you do a word search of a name there are several things you will want to keep in mind.

1. Make sure the name refers to the person you are studying. (There are five men called John, eight men called Judas, fifteen men called Jonathan, and thirty men called Zechariah!)

2. Take into consideration multiple names for the same person. This may include a secondary Hebrew or Greek name. For example, Esther was also called Hadassah (her Hebrew name), and Shadrach, Meshach, and Abednego, were also known as Hananiah, Mishael, and Azariah. It may also include names that were changed, such as Sarai, which was later changed to Sarah. And remember, Jacob was also called Israel, as was the entire nation of his descendants!

It is difficult to limit this study to a defined parameter (chapter or book) because all of the facts about the person's life that are given in the Bible need to be considered and, quite possibly, this will involve several books in the Bible. However, the initial stages of gathering information can be limited to one book or passage of the Bible. If you decide to proceed with this plan of progressive research, always take time to organize the data you have collected in one passage or book before moving on to another.

Collect

Depending on the person you have chosen to study, you will have a minimal or a massive amount of material to gather. As you read and do word searches these are the types of questions you will want to answer.

Questions for Studying a Biography:

1. **WHO** is the person? Note attitudes, philosophies, motives, spiritual status, character traits, assets, and liabilities. Who are other significant people—contemporaries, friends, colaborers, enemies, etc.?

---

2. **WHAT** is the role of this person in the Bible? Note actions, events, ministry, occupation, training, achievements, contributions, writings, influence, crises, etc.

3. **WHEN** did this person live and minister? Note the historical setting, political conditions, religious conditions, and other time elements related to events and experiences in his or her life. Note the time span of the individual's life and when he or she died.

4. **WHERE** did significant events take place? Note places of birth, travels, ministry, trials, conflicts, spiritual struggles or victories, etc.

5. **WHY** is each fact included? How is it important? How did it affect this individual or others?

As you search through the Scriptures to answer these questions, think of the process as a personality interview. That means that **no** detail is trivial. You will want to consider the characteristics of **all** people who interacted with the major personality as you will want to research **every** place and event that is mentioned. Like a good interviewer, try to remain objective and unbiased. Do not let your own opinions or experiences affect your observations, and do not shy away from the negative side of the person's life— the errors, sins, mistakes, and foolishness. Remember the old saying, "We cannot really know a person unless we know them warts and all."

As you would with an actual interview, be sure to include what other people have said about the individual. This can provide keen insights into the personality you are studying.

Throughout the process of gathering this data, if the information you have found is worded awkwardly or seems inconsistent, compare the Bible text with another or several other translations. Very likely this will clarify the information.

Of course, the final objective in collecting the data is to observe not only what factors influenced this person's life but to understand how they influenced that life. For example, when we observe a fault, we want to go beyond merely identifying the fault to understanding its causes and its results, not only upon the individual but also upon others.

Organize

One of the most obvious, yet effective, methods of organizing information about an individual is to develop a chronology of his or her life. Simply write out all pertinent experiences, events, situations, etc., in the order they occurred. The benefit of organizing the material in such a historical time-line chart is that it brings into clear view any overall patterns of progression, development, or decline. It allows you to see how experiences in the person's life were interwoven in the positive or negative development of his or her character.

For example, if we considered a chronological chart of David's life we would see how from the initial triumph of his coronation he fell tragically into sin, and only after years of great sorrow and suffering did he finally experience restoration.

As another example, consider the categories of Job's life that Irving Jensen (*Simply Understanding the Bible*, World Wide Pub.; Minneapolis, MN: 1990) suggests:

Job is Tested	chapters 1 and 2
Job Despairs	chapter 3
Job is Counseled	chapters 4–37
Job is Approved	chapters 38–42

To help you develop a chronological chart, look for:

- climactic points in the person's life
- major phases or episodes in the person's life
- obvious changes of attitude
- time boundaries

Consider

Biographical Bible study translates truth in terms of life—it illustrates truth through personal examples. Our goal in this study is not only to distinguish the principles that affected one life in the Bible, but to define biblical principles that apply to our lives as well. Ultimately, we want to know more than facts about a life—we want to know why those facts were included in the Bible. We want to grasp the significance of that life to biblical teaching.

When you have organized the biographical information into a chart, graph, or outline, use this to:

1. Perform a character analysis.
2. Determine character development or decline.
3. Identify biblical principles.

To perform a character analysis, you will want to distinguish negative or positive traits in this person's life. Decide which incidents from his or her life illustrate each trait. If possible, trace its causes and its results (upon the individual and upon others). Also, observe how these traits influenced decisions, how they affected others, and how they helped the person face life and overcome obstacles.

If you have developed your material chronologically, it will be fairly easy to identify character development or decline. Notice changes in behavior and philosophy and summarize the effects of these changes both upon the individual and upon others.

Generally, after you have described the character traits of the individual and have determined a pattern of progression or digression, the applicable spiritual principles and truths will be obvious. In this context, look particularly for divine interaction with the individual, relationships with God and with other believers, etc.

Here are some questions to ask as you consider the information gathered in a biographic study:

1. How does this life exemplify biblical truths?
2. Does this life serve as an example? A warning?
3. What sentence best describes this person?
4. What are some long-term results of his or her life?
5. Which of his or her character traits should I seek to develop in my life?
6. Which character traits should I avoid?
7. What was this person's greatest accomplishment? Greatest error?

Apply

Probably no other method of Bible study is so easy to apply personally as the biographical method. Observing character traits and their far-reaching effects on a life can serve as a powerful motivation to develop the positive traits in our lives or to delete the negative traits if they are present. The lives of Bible characters serve as examples to us. They can warn us what to avoid, and they can encourage us to do even more than we dared!

A Biographical Study in Philippians

Exploring and Collecting Data

There are several individuals mentioned in the book of Philippians, and while Paul would have been a natural choice, we decided to study the life of Timothy. We also decided to limit the parameter of our study, at least initially, to the book of Philippians.

To collect data about Timothy, we performed a word search and answered the following questions.

1. **Who is the person and who are other significant people?**

We searched for the name Timothy, but in the King James Version there was no reference to this name in Philippians. In this version he is referred to as Timotheus, and a search of that name indicated the following information:

direct reference–2 verses, 1:1 and 2:19
indirect reference–4 verses, 2:20–23

Paul refers to Timothy as his "son," an expression Paul used to refer to those he had led to Christ. Timothy is also called a servant with Paul in the Gospel. In these references we were not given any information about Timothy's background. We would need to search in other books for this information. But we did find several clues to his attitudes and character traits.

Timothy is described as:

committed to Christ   1:1, 2:21

concerned for others   2:20

a responsible worker   2:22

a preacher of the Gospel 2:22

a compassionate friend   2:22

a cooperative minister   2:22

The other significant person mentioned is, of course, Paul. In these few verses we noted a close relationship between these two individuals. Paul had led Timothy to Christ, and now Timothy was helping Paul during his time of imprisonment. Timothy was preaching the Gospel and was agreeable to Paul's request that he return to Philippi to help the church there. This relationship revealed Timothy's attitudes of submission, care, responsibility, and selflessness.

2. What is the role of this person?

In these passages we have a picture of Timothy working as Paul's right-hand man. Not only did he care for Paul, but together with Paul he was sending the letter to the Philippians, and he was busy preaching the Gospel in Rome. Paul speaks highly of Timothy and his work. At Paul's request, Timothy is returning to minister in the church at Philippi.

3. When did this person live and minister?

By searching through a concordance and a Bible dictionary we were able to pinpoint the time of this letter to A.D. 61–62, during Paul's initial imprisonment in Rome under house arrest. We also discovered that the church in Philippi began around A.D. 50, on Paul's second missionary journey. At the time this letter was written it was a thriving church.

If we had extended the parameters of our search to include other books, we would have found information about other periods of Timothy's life.

4. Where did significant events take place?

The setting is Rome, when Paul was under house arrest. Timothy was there with Paul, caring for him and preaching the Gospel. Paul states that Timothy will soon be visiting the church in Philippi.

5. **Why are these facts included in the letter?**

Timothy is mentioned initially as sending the letter with Paul. They were working together in Rome and shared in the spirit of this letter if not in the actual writing. Paul wants the Philippians to know of Timothy's concern for them and wants to inform them that Timothy will be coming to see them again soon and will minister to them.

Organizing the Data

We summarized the facts about Timothy's life into the following chart:

Timothy in Philippians	
Birth and Early Life	(no information given in Philippians)
Conversion and call	Conversion through Paul 2:22
	Committed to Christ 1:1
Ministry	Christ centered 1:1, 2:20, 21
	Co-laborer with Paul 1:1, 2:19, 20, 22
	Preached gospel 2:22
	Paul's messenger 2:19, 23
	Trouble shooter 2:20
	Respected by Paul 2:20-22
	Entrusted with Responsibility 2:19, 20
	Good reputation 2:22
Character	Dedicated to Christ 1:1, 2:21
	Sincere 2:20
	Selfless 2:21
	Compassionate 2:20
	Responsible 2:20
	Cooperative 2:22
	Submissive 2:22

Relationship with Others	Junior associate of Paul
	Respected church leader 2:20–22
	Soon to visit and minister in Philippi 2:23
Death	(no information given in Phillippians)
Reason for Facts Given	Preparation for his visit to Philippi

 Considering the Data

As we organized the information about Timothy, several positive character traits stood out.

1. He was **dedicated**: not only to Paul but also to the work of the Lord.

2. He was **sincere**: he was sincerely concerned for both Paul and the church at Philippi.

3. He was **selfless**: his life was not spent in pursuit of personal gain or pleasure but rather in helping others, ministering, and preaching the gospel.

4. He was **compassionate**: he genuinely cared about other people.

5. He was **responsible**: not only in his attitudes toward others but in his work of preaching and his willingness to travel again to Philippi.

6. He was **cooperative**: he had worked for many years with Paul in the ministry. Paul speaks highly of him in this regard.

7. He was **submissive**: he was willing to work under the authority of Paul and to go where Paul felt it was necessary for the sake of the Gospel.

With Paul being under house arrest, the working conditions in Rome were probably difficult, yet Timothy stayed there as a faithful friend and colaborer to care for Paul and to preach the Gospel. He was concerned about the work of the Lord, and he was concerned about others. Timothy was certainly an admirable person!

To determine what biblical truths we could learn from this information about Timothy we answered the application questions. Some of our answers included:

1. Without doubt, Timothy serves as a wonderful example not only to all believers but particularly to associate ministers or those who work for God under the authority of another.

2. Timothy's life was an illustration of God's selfless love and concern for others.

3. We know that as a result of Timothy's life, Paul's ministry was enhanced and enlarged. Research elsewhere would probably confirm that Timothy had a positive long-term effect on the Philippian church.

Making Application

It would be difficult not to be impressed with Timothy. His life was a wonderful example of Christian character. After completing this study we felt motivated to develop some of his character traits. For example:

- We need to be willing to minister with another in an attitude of submission. This could involve assisting with a Sunday school class or helping with the youth activities. It would probably require lots of hard work with very little gratitude or rewards.

- We need to become concerned about other believers to the point that we are willing to make personal sacrifices for their welfare.

- We need to be faithful to responsibilities.

Where to Go from Here

Our study is only a modest introduction to the life of Timothy. Much additional information about his life is available by searching through the rest of the New Testament.

Other individuals mentioned in the book of Philippians that would be interesting to study are:

Epaphroditus

Euodia

Syntyche

Paul

While you probably would not find too much information on the first three individuals, Philippians would provide ample data about Paul! In Philippians 3:1–8 Paul gives an autobiographical sketch of his life prior to his conversion to emphasize the dramatic change brought about by that conversion. This could serve as the first phase of a study of his life throughout all of his writings.

Chapter Thirteen

From Eden to Patmos:
Computer Historical-Geographical Study

> ". . . Let your glory be over all
> the earth."
> Psalm 57:11 (NCV)

T he Bible is a book about *people:* a woman making bread, a man fishing, a baby in a basket, a king fighting battles, a man swimming in a river to be healed. It is a book about *places:* a fortress that fell when trumpets blasted, a mountain where God gave the Law, a village that housed the infant king of kings, a lake where a man walked on the water. It is a book about *property:* a tent, a sling shot, a stone waterpot, a vineyard—all existing in a culture and time removed from ours by hundreds of centuries. To understand the Bible, and to correctly interpret what it says, we need to understand the history, culture, geography, and politics of ancient Bible times. We need to read and study the message from the perspective of the original writer and the recipients or those discussed in the text.

This is the purpose of the historical-geographical method of Bible study: to reconstruct the historical-geographical setting as closely as possible and understand the text from that perspective. It is a procedure of gathering information about the people, places, objects, and events of Bible times. These facts and details then provide insight into the background or framework of a passage, a chapter, or perhaps even an entire book, which in turn helps us to correctly interpret the truths in that passage, chapter, or book.

For example, to understand the book of Daniel, you would want to gather information about King Nebuchadnezzar and the political systems of that day. You would also want to research the city of Babylon, and you would want to be aware of the time period of this book in relationship to the chronology of Israel.

Performing a Historical-Geographical Study

In this study, you can arbitrarily choose a subject from the myriad geographic, political, cultural, and historical details in the Bible. However, a historical study is usually performed as a component of the study of a specific passage or book. For example, although someone might be interested in gathering information about the ancient town of Laodicea, it is more likely that they would want to have this data if they were studying the passage in Revelation 3 that refers to the Laodicean church as being "luke-warm." Indeed, geographical information about this town indicates that it was located near both a hot spring and a cold spring, and that although a conduit system brought water into the city from both springs, by the time it reached the city it was neither cold nor hot—it was simply lukewarm. Not only is such information inter-esting, it is also helps us appreciate the appropriateness of this description of the Laodicean church.

When you know what historical factor you want to study, begin by performing a word search through your electronic text for additional occurrences of the person, place, object, or event. Search first in the immediate environment, then in other parts of that book, and finally in other books of the Bible. As you perform the search, pay attention to related subjects that can provide further information.

For example, when you are gathering data about a town, you will also want to look for information about the province, country, or empire in which the town was located. When a person or event is mentioned in conjunction with your topic, research other passages of Scripture for information on the person and locate references that recount the event. This means that when you study the epistles, you will want to search through the book of Acts for information about the historical setting and development of each church and for facts about individual converts or members of the church. When you are looking for historical information about a person, place, or event in one Gospel, the other three Gospels can serve as a prime source for additional details. In the Old Testament, the primary historical books are a good source of background information. These are: Genesis, Exodus, Numbers, Joshua, Judges, 1 and 2 Samuel, 1 and 2 Kings, Ezra, and Nehemiah.

Throughout the process of performing word searches for historical information, it can be helpful to compare the Scripture references indicated in your translation with other translations. Sometimes contemporary translations offer additional historical and geographical insights.

In addition to your work with the electronic text, you can take advantage of other tools developed specifically to provide historical-geographical information, such as:

- a Bible Dictionary
- a Bible encyclopedia
- a Bible Atlas

These supplementary resources, available in an electronic medium, can instantly place a wealth of information at your fingertips.

Collect

The data you will want to collect in this method of study can be divided into four basic categories: history, geography, culture, and politics. Here are some suggestions for compiling information in each category.

History. Someone once said, "The Bible is a history book, and you can't understand it unless you understand history." That is why the time you spend researching Bible history with your computer will be an invaluable help in understanding God's Word.

The objective in this type of research is to become familiar with events in biblical history and to understand both how they fit in with the basic chronology of events either in the Old Testament or in the New Testament and how they relate to major events and persons in global world history. Much of the research for this study will involve finding information about related events in earlier times or in subsequent secular history and discovering facts about the origins of places, things, and events.

Some of the questions you will want to ask in gathering data for this area of study are listed below.

Questions for a Historical Study

1. Where did this event occur?

2. What caused this event?

3. When did this event occur?

4. Who was involved in this event?

5. How did this event affect the people involved?

6. Where does the event fit in the Old or New Testament chronology?

7. What significant historical events occurred in world history at the same time?

8. What is the significance of this event to God's people?

Geography. Too often we are tempted to skim over geographical details in the Bible, probably because we do not realize that they can shed significant light on the meaning of a passage of Scripture. For instance, we read in the Gospels that Mary and Joseph traveled from Nazareth to Bethlehem just prior to the birth of Jesus. The journey between the two towns does not have much significance until we do some geographic research and learn that Bethlehem was located on a mountain ridge eighty-five miles south of Nazareth, which was also located in a mountainous area. Thus, in order to make this trip, the couple would have traveled down the mountain from Nazareth into the Jordan Valley; then they would have walked approximately fifty miles along the valley; after that they would have ascended the mountain ridge up to Jerusalem; and from there would have proceeded on south another five miles along the mountain ridge to the town of Bethlehem—all of this walking along dusty roads or riding on the back of a donkey. Considering the distance, and Mary's condition, they were probably on the road for several weeks—estimates range from three weeks to three months. An arduous undertaking even for the physically-fit carpenter Joseph, it must have been extremely challenging for young Mary in her final weeks of pregnancy.

Can you see how the facts of the geographic setting add immeasurably to our understanding of the event of Christ's birth? We need to develop a habit of asking questions about even trivial details of geology and topology. Here are some questions you might want to ask.

Questions for a Geographical Study

1. Where is it located?
2. What is the topography of the region?
3. What is the climate?
4. What distances are involved?
5. What are noteworthy features about the area?
6. How do these factors affect the people involved?
7. How do they shed light on the meaning of the Scriptures?

As you gather the information that answers these questions, create a file for each location or topographical feature. Then you can draw on these files to implement future geographic research.

Culture. Many things in the Bible seem strange to us. Others are downright puzzling basically because we are not familiar with the lifestyles of the people who lived in Bible times. Their habits of living were so different from ours! Their clothing was different, their food was different, their houses were different, as were their professions, weapons, tools, musical instruments, architecture, art, religious ceremonies, methods of transportation, and so forth. Not only did they live in a culture remarkably distinct from ours, but they lived in a culture centuries older than ours!

How can we understand a culture so far removed from ours? First, we have to inform ourselves about the culture. As we gather facts and details about customs, clothing, traditions, and laws we will gather understanding: about the people of the Bible, about their experiences, and about their relationship with God. In this computer study we want to identify cultural factors, and we want to explain their significance to a correct understanding of Scripture.

For example, if we were studying the life of Matthew, we would want to research the profession of a tax collector. We would use our computer programs to find information about the practice of tax collecting, about the history of tax collecting, and about the relationship between Jewish tax collectors and the imperial government of that time. Then we would want to decide how the background of being a tax collector might have affected Matthew and his role as a disciple.

In this study, the most profitable questions will be those your own curiosity initiates, but here are some suggestions to help you get started:

Questions for a Cultural Study

1. What is the custom or cultural factor?
2. What aspect of life did it affect—physical, spiritual, mental?
3. How did it affect that aspect of life?
4. How did it affect the value system of those involved?
5. How did it develop?
6. What were the reasons for it?
7. What factors in the environment are interrelated with it?
8. Are there contemporary equivalents?
9. What is the significance of this factor to the meaning of Scripture?

Politics. Nations, governments, kings, and emperors are woven throughout the Bible story. Numerous political systems affected the lives of people in the Old Testament and in the New Testament. If we are going to understand the Bible, we need to be familiar with the politics of Bible times. We need to be familiar with how kingdoms and nations developed and how they fit in with God's purpose for His people.

One of the keys to understanding the political climate of a certain period of time is to gather information about the nations of that time such as Egypt, Assyria, Babylon, Persia, Greece, or Rome.

Through your computer study in this category you will also want to gather information about rulers: their strengths and weaknesses, who they conquered, and who defeated them. You will want to know about governments: about the hierarchy of authority and power, about friends and enemies, and about boundaries of control or influence. Ultimately you want to determine how the political system or ruler affected an individual or a group of people in the Bible.

When you are doing a historical Bible study, you will also want to consult sources of secular history. As you gather information about political systems, here are some questions you might want to ask:

Questions for a Political Study

1. What nation was in power?
2. What are some positive and negative characteristics of the nation?
3. How long was it in power?
4. How was it defeated?
5. Where does the political system fit in the chronology of the Bible?
6. Who was the king, emperor, or ruler of the nation?
7. How did this political system affect the people of God?

Organize

Collecting data in a historical-geographical study can be confusing unless you take care to keep the information that is pertinent to each category in a separate file, either on note paper or in a computer file. Admittedly, in some instances the information may overlap categories, but in this case record the facts in both categories. In other words, if you discover that a distinctive chariot was used in a particular battle, you will probably want to record this information in both a culture category-file and a political category-file.

This study lends itself to multiple types of graphs. The details you gather can be presented by basic categories or subcategories;

by relevance to a particular text regardless of category; by events, items, or people in a particular period of time, and so forth.

Another way to organize historical-geographical data is to write a description of the historical situation reflected by the passage. If you are working with an epistle, write what was going on in the writer's life that led him to write the letter. Describe the relationship between the author and the recipients of the letter, both prior to the letter and at the time the letter was written. In a historical narrative, describe the historical scene and the characters involved. These descriptions will help you understand the scriptural principles behind the written text.

 Consider

Of all the methods of Bible study we have presented, this may seem the most difficult in terms of finding biblical principles that are applicable for believers today. But even when we consider tools and foods and lakes and emperors, we can find spiritual truths. The key is to remember these three steps:

1. Find information about the historical feature.
2. Determine the significance of that historical feature to the text.
3. Determine how that significance relates to the believer today.

In other words, we want to find out what the Passover was— that is how it originated and what customs and food were involved with it—then we want to clarify how these factors were significant to Christ's final Passover with his disciples, and based on this information we want to identify spiritual truths for our lives today. Questions that can help to distinguish these spiritual truths include:

1. How were their lives like our lives?
2. How did their lives differ from our lives?
3. Does the historical factor relate directly to doctrinal issues? Indirectly?
4. What doctrinal issues are involved?
5. How did the historical factor affect the spiritual development of God's people? The church?

6. Does this have any effect on the lives of believers today?

7. What can I learn from this historical factor that will benefit my spiritual life?

8. How was God at work?

9. How does this information help me understand the passage or book?

 Apply

Although you will be studying concrete facts and figures in this method, do not let that rob you of the opportunity to find biblical truths that will help you in your relationship with God. A key to making personal application from this study is to note how the historical factor affected or influenced people's lives, and then find a lesson that you can learn from their experiences. Put yourself in their shoes—try to understand the passage from their perspective and value system. The answers to the questions given above will also help you to make personal application of the historical data.

A Historical-Geographical Study in Philippians

Exploring and Collecting the Data

In this third method of study we researched material from the book of Philippians that was pertinent to four basic categories: geography, history, culture, and politics. We performed word searches in our online text for words indicating people, places such as Macedonia and Philippi, and things. We also consulted an online atlas and Bible dictionary. We used the questions suggested for each category as a guide in our explorations. Here, in brief, is the information we gathered.

History

1. The church at Philippi began when Paul received a vision and a call to go to Macedonia. (Acts 16:9–12)

2. Paul first preached to a group of women (Jewish proselytes) who met by the river to pray. One of these women, Lydia, became the first convert. Her entire household also accepted the Gospel. (Acts 16:13–15)

3. Paul cast an evil spirit out of a slave girl who practiced some form of divination. (Acts 16:16–18)

4. The owners of the slave girl were angered, and they incited the wrath of the townspeople against Paul and his companion, Silas. (Acts 16:19–21)

5. The two men were beaten and put in an inner prison with their feet in stocks. (Acts 16:22–24)

6. In spite of their ill treatment, Paul and Silas sang hymns and gave thanks. In the middle of the night an earthquake loosed the chains of the prisoners, and although all were free, no one fled. (Acts 16:25–26)

7. Due to the testimony of Paul and Silas, the jailer and his family accepted the Gospel. (Acts 16:27–34)

8. When the magistrates learned that Paul and Silas were Roman citizens, they feared reprisals for the beatings and imprisonment, so they begged them to leave the city immediately. (Acts 16:35–40)

9. Paul visited the church on numerous occasions, and Timothy served here as a minister. (Acts 19:22)

10. This was known as Paul's favorite church. (Phil. 1:7, 8)

11. The church at Philippi was a generous church. Although the believers there were poor themselves, they gave generously to help the poor in Jerusalem, and they supported Paul on his missionary journeys—twice when he was at Thessalonica, once when he was at Corinth, and again on the occasion of this letter when he was imprisoned in Rome. (Romans 15:25–26, Phil. 4:16–18)

12. The church sent Epaphroditus, one of their members, to stay and care for Paul. He got sick, and when the church heard about this they were upset. He heard that they were worried for his sake, and this upset him. (Phil. 2:25–30)

Geography

1. Philippi, a city in the province of Macedonia, was located just north of the port of Neapolis on the Aegean Sea, in the plain east of Mt. Pangaeus. A major center of trade and commerce on

the road system of northern Greece, it was known as the gateway to the East. It is not surprising that Paul's first convert here was a woman who traded a type of purple garment for which the region was famous.

2. This was the first European city that Paul visited, and it served throughout the remainder of his travels as a strategic location for his missionary journeys.

Culture

Prison System:

1. The prisons of Paul's time were sordid, dank caves or deep holes.

2. The inner areas, which were the most vile and filthy, were reserved for the worst criminals.

3. Guards or jailers who allowed prisoners to escape were killed.

4. In some instances, if a prisoner had status and money he would be allowed to rent lodgings while remaining under house arrest. Paul was in such a situation when Epaphroditus brought him the financial help from the church at Philippi.

5. Undoubtedly, due to Paul's initial experience in prison in Philippi, and the fact that one of the converts was a jailer, this church wanted to make sure Paul had sufficient finances so he did not have to forego the more comfortable prison of house arrest.

Women:

1. History records that this province accorded status to women not shown in other areas.

2. Women were involved in trade and commerce outside of their homes, an unusual custom for the culture of the time.

3. It is not surprising that women play a prominent role in the church here.

Politics

1. The people of Philippi were conquered by the Romans in 168 B.C.

2. In 42 B.C., the forces of Octavius and Anthony defeated the forces of the Roman republic here.

3. After the victory of 42 B.C., some of the Roman soldiers were ordered to remain living in that area. Thus, Philippi became known as a garrison town, and many soldiers came there to retire.

4. As a result of the victory of 42 B.C., the city of Philippi was designated a miniature Rome, and its residents were given unique citizenship privileges.

5. The citizens of Philippi enjoyed the full rights of Roman citizenship including exemption from taxes.

6. This explains why the magistrates were fearful when they found out they had beaten two Roman citizens, Paul and Silas. (Acts 16:37–39)

7. It also explains why Paul refers to citizenship in his letter—in 3:20.

Organizing the Data

We condensed the material into a simple graph with three categories of historical information and the significance of that information to the book of Philippians.

Historical Information about Philippians

	Location	People	Politics
Historical Information	European City; Cross-roads of trade between East and West; Garrison town; Excellent roads	Trade/commerce; High status for women locally	Roman citizenship
Significance to Epistle	Strategic location for missionary journeys; Paul, Timothy, and others stayed here or travelled through here on their missionary journeys	Believers were generous givers; Women highly involved in the church	Believers were "citizens of heaven"

Considering the Data

After gathering historical facts about the town of Philippi and some aspects of the culture, we determined the significance of those facts to the book of Philippians. Here are some of our observations:

1. In light of Paul's dreadful prison experience in Philippi, and the fact that one of the earliest church members was a jailer, it is not surprising that this church wanted to send money to Paul to make his life in prison as comfortable as possible. They had first-hand information the hardships of prison life.

2. Paul's first convert in Philippi was a woman, Lydia. Although the Jews did not have a synagogue in this town, Lydia, along with other women, met by the river to pray on the Sabbath. This is where Paul first encountered them. Lydia was a career woman, involved in selling garments of purple. Women in this region were given higher status than in other provinces, so it is not surprising that we see a strong involvement of women in this church. In fact, Paul's only rebuke in the letter is to two women who were having trouble getting along with each other.

3. The citizens of Philippi were proud of their Roman citizenship. This was a distinction of honor for their city in the entire region. Paul alludes to this privilege when he speaks of citizenship in heaven. These were words the Philippian believers would readily understand!

Making Application

After deciding how the historical facts related to the book of Philippians, we considered how that significance might relate to our lives. These are some of our conclusions:

1. The Philippian believers were not only generous, they were also compassionate. They serve as examples for us to empathize with individuals who face difficult situations that we are familiar with or perhaps have even experienced ourselves.

2. Do we act like we are proud to be "citizens of heaven"? Or do we take it for granted? As it was a privilege for the Philippians to be considered Roman citizens, so we need to remember what a high honor and privilege it is for us to be "citizens of heaven."

Where to Go from Here

If you would like to do further historical studies from the book of Philippians, you might consider these suggestions:

The routes of Paul's missionary journeys

The Roman Government of Paul's day

Local religions

Chapter Fourteen

In Touch with Topics:
Computer Topical Study

". . . the earth will be full of the
knowledge of the LORD as the
waters cover the sea."
Isaiah 11:9 (NRSV)

here is an old saying: "Before you borrow money from a friend, decide which you need most." Fortunately, deciding which Bible topic to study is much less complicated for there is hardly a topic of thought or conversation that is not treated in the Bible—be it marital fidelity, fish, or fanaticism. Regardless of the topic, if you are interested in it, you can probably find it in the Bible! Topics include subjects (objects, attitudes, qualities, attributes), themes, doctrines, arguments, controversies, and so forth. In fact, a topic can include several themes or subjects.

In some instances, to avoid feeling overwhelmed by data and information, you may want to concentrate your studies on one aspect of a topic at a time. For example, the topic of "Prayer," could include numerous themes or subtopics including "Prayers of Jesus," "Methods of Prayer," "Conditions for Answered Prayer," etc. The best way to study an extensive topic like this is to research and analyze one theme or subtopic at a time. When you feel satisfied with your efforts on that theme, you can move on to another theme.

Performing A Topical Study

Explore

Decide what topic you want to study in the Bible and establish the boundaries for your study. Initially, it is advisable to limit the scope of your study both in physical parameters within the Bible (a chapter, a portion of a book, or a small book) and in the spectrum of your topic, particularly if it is complex. Once you have completed compiling information within that range you could increase the boundaries to include other chapters, books, etc., and other facets of the topic.

To study a topic you will want to gather information about both direct and indirect references to the topic. So after you have selected your topic, make a list of terms or phrases that are associated with the topic including attributes, characteristics, individuals, places, synonyms, antonyms, etc. These will become part of your research material. (If you are not sure what terms or phrases would be relevant to the topic you have chosen, you can find this information in an exhaustive concordance or topical Bible.)

As you can see, a topical study is more involved than a word study, because in addition to searching for the basic word you will also want to search for words, phrases, or strings of words that relate to the topic. For example, if you choose to study the theme of "thanksgiving" you will want to search first for the word *thanksgiving;* then you will search for related words such as *praise, adoration,* and *thankfulness;* finally, you will want to search for phrases such as "giving thanks," "making a joyful noise," "joyful songs," "songs of praise," etc. It can also be beneficial to include synonyms or antonyms in this study. For example, a study of *love* would include exploring the concept of *hate* or *bitterness.*

By using the wildcard search capability on your computer, you will find that the extended word searches that are necessary for a topical study can be completed quickly and effortlessly. Wildcards expand the scope of a simple word search to include auxiliary words or phrases. For example, as part of the research for the topic of *love,* a wildcard search with **love*** would include the words *love, loved, lovest, lovely, lovesick, lovers,* etc. This search would supply a much larger group of references to explore than a simple search of *love.*

Collect

What kind of data do you want to collect when performing a topical study? Remember, in a topical study you will want to compile information about the key word or phrase as well as the secondary words and phrases. And while you will probably want to limit your study initially to a restricted passage, chapter, or book, topical studies generally require gathering information from multiple passages, chapters, books, and even across testaments. You will probably want to begin with a search of the root word of your study and from there expand to searches for words and phrases that are related to the subject.

We suggest you use the following questions as a guideline for gathering information about a topic. Perform searches of words and phrases as necessary to answer the questions and record your answers either on a piece of paper or in a computer file.

Questions for Studying a Topic

1. Where do direct references to the topic occur?
2. What other words or similar phrases will provide information on this topic?
3. Where do these words or phrases occur?
4. Is the topic defined or explained?
5. Is the topic illustrated, compared, or contrasted?
6. What are the meanings of key terms?
7. Is it apparent that various authors present the topic with a distinct emphasis?
8. What are key passages on the topic that could be used to teach it?

 Organize

Because the topical study includes broader areas for searches than the word study, you will be working with larger amounts of material. To begin this study you will want to print out the Scripture references you discovered in the process of doing word and phrase searches with sufficient text to give you the whole idea that is expressed in the references. Then, to make the optimum use of these references you will want to:

- observe relationships between the references
- categorize these relationships
- summarize key ideas
- define some of the key words

At this stage of your study, concentrate on sorting the material into categories with precise labels. It is likely that initially you will have rather broad categories with numerous references in each. If so, you might want to sort through the categories again, looking for subcategories of more restricted associations between items in the categories. Once you have developed tightly structured categories (and subcategories), use these as the basis for creating a chart or graph. Or perhaps you will simply want to record the title of each category or subcategory in outline form.

 Consider

Once the material has been categorized and organized, you will want to determine what spiritual truths can be uncovered from your studies of this topic. To help you distinguish these truths we suggest you answer questions like those given below. Use these questions as a springboard to create additional questions of your own.

1. Does the topic include information about basic Bible doctrine?
2. Does the study reveal characteristics of the Christian life?
3. What promises or provisions are indicated?
4. Are responsibilities indicated for believers?
5. Are there words of encouragement and hope?
6. What sentence summarizes the findings of this study?
7. What is the most important aspect of this study for my life?

Apply

Based on your answers to the foregoing questions, make a list of principles and truths that are relevant to your life situation and describe how you could take steps to implement them. Take care to consider the context of these principles and verify that they are applicable across time and space. Some biblical principles and commands are prescriptive not descriptive. That is, they were given to a particular person or group of people in a particular situation, they are not given to all people for all time.

A Topical Study in Philippians

Exploring and Collecting the Data

In our previous readings of the book of Philippians we noticed one topic that occurred frequently was "God," so we decided to do a topical study on the doctrine of God. Obviously this is a topic that could include nearly every page of the Bible, so we chose to limit our study at this point to the book of Philippians. To compile information on this topic, we answered the following questions:

1. **Where do direct references to the topic occur?**

A search of the word *God* indicated that it occurred in twenty-three verses:

6 verses in chapter 1

7 verses in chapter 2

4 verses in chapter 3

6 verses in chapter 4

We copied each of these verses into our computer file.

2. **What other words or similar phrases will provide information on this topic?**

Other words and phrases that we searched for were:

Father -	4 verses
glory -	5 verses
glory of God -	2 verses
worship -	1 verse
righteousness -	3 verses
kingdom of God -	none
heavenly Father -	none
Jehovah -	none

3. Where do these words or phrases occur?

Some of the verses with these related words and phrases of course overlapped with our original listing of verses containing the word *God*. We made note of all references in our "doctrine of God" file.

Father	glory	glory of God	worship	righteousness
1:2	1:11	1:11	3:3	1:11
2:11	2:11	2:11		3:6
4:20	3:19			3:9
	4:19			
	4:20			

4. Is the topic defined or explained?

Although we did not find a definition per se of *God,* we did find that God is described through titles, attributes, and actions. Note for example:

Concordance Entry	Attribute	Concordance Entry	Title
3:15	omniscient	1:2	God our Father
2:27	merciful	2:11	God the Father
3:9	righteous	4:9	God of Peace
3:3	triune	4:20	God and Father
2:13, 4:19	omnipotent	1:8, 14, 28	God
4:20	eternal		
2:9	sovereign		

Concordance Entry	Acts
1:2	gives grace
1:2	gives peace
1:3, 4	hears our prayers
1:6	works in us
1:8	knows how we feel
1:28	provides salvation
2:9	exalted Christ
2:9	gave Christ his name
2:13	works in us
3:3	is to be worshiped
3:9	is the source of righteousness
3:15	reveals things to us
4:6	hears our requests
4:9	is with us
4:18	accepts sacrifices
4:19	supplies our needs

5. Is the topic illustrated, compared, or contrasted?

The divine nature of God was *illustrated* through his actions, titles, and acts as mentioned above.

God is *compared* (as being equal) with the other members of the trinity—the Spirit and Jesus Christ:

- common work — God our Father and Jesus Christ linked in providing grace and peace (1:2)
- common nature — Christ in the form of God (2:6)
- members of Godhead — equality with God (2:6)
  a. Spirit of God (3:3)
  b. Father (1:2, 2:11, 4:20)
  c. Lord, Jesus Christ (1:2, 2:11)

We noted three **contrasts** from our data:

* as opposed to the darkness of the world, the sons of God shine as lights in a crooked and perverse world (2:15)
* the righteousness which is of God is contrasted with the righteousness of the law (3:9)
* as opposed to the true God, the god of those who are enemies of the cross of Christ is their appetites; their mind is on earthly things (3:19)

6. What are the meanings of key terms?

We looked in our electronic Bible dictionary (Strong's) to find definitions for key words in our group of references.

God = (*thĕŏs*) supreme divinity

mercy = (*ĕlĕĕŏ*) compassion, forbearance, have compassion or pity

grace = (*charis*) grant as a favor, pardon, rescue, graciousness

peace = (*ĕirēnē*) tranquility, quietness, rest, lack of discord

witness = (*martus*) testimony, martyr, record

righteousness = (*dikaiŏsunē*) equity, justification, being just

glory = (*dŏxa*) dignity, honor, praise, worship

salvation = (*sōtēria*) rescue, safety, deliverance

equality = (*isŏs*) like, similar, as much

will = (*thĕlō*) to choose, to determine

work = (*ĕnĕrgĕō*) to be active, to accomplish, mighty

riches = (*plŏutŏs*) fullness, abundance, valuable bestowment

7. Is it apparent that various authors present the topic with a distinct emphasis?

Because we had limited our study to the book of Philippians we did not study the writings of other authors.

Organizing the Data

We organized the Scripture references into categories according to similarities or patterns in content. Then we developed charts for the categories.

1. In the first chart we wanted to organize the material that described the divine essence of God. As you can see we divided the chart into two classifications: Who God is—His Character; and What He Does—His actions.

2. While organizing the verses that contained the word *God,* we noted several references to "things" of God, for example "children of God" and "peace of God." We thought it would be helpful to place these items in a separate chart. In the process, we noticed that three of these were contrasted in the text, so we included this in the chart.

WHO GOD IS —His Character		WHAT GOD DOES —His Actions	
Attributes	**Titles**	**Interacts with Humanity**	**Interacts with Trinity**
merciful	God our Father	provides: grace	exalts Christ
righteous	God the Father	peace	gave Christ name
triune	God of Peace	salvation	Spirit of God
omniscient	God and Father	mercy	equal to all
omnipotent	God	righteousness	
eternal		hears our prayers	
		works in our lives	
		knows our feelings	
		is pleased with sacrifices	
		is to be worshiped	
		reveals truth to us	
		is present with us	
		heals	
		supplies our needs	

Descriptions of Things of God		
Children of God	——contrasted to——	**Enemies of Christ**
blameless		end is destruction
innocent		ruled by physical appetites
above reproach		
lights in a dark world		proud of shamefulness
hold fast the Word		minds set on worldly things
Peace of God		**Anxiety**
surpasses all comprehension		
guards our hearts and minds		
Righteousness of God		**Righteousness of Law**
through faith in Christ		through self
Word of God		
proclaims Christ		
is Word of Life		

 Considering the Data

We looked through the material on the graphs and all the references in our file to answer the questions suggested earlier. Some of our observations are listed below.

1. There is much information in these passages about the nature of God. This would comprise the doctrine of God. There is also some reference to the Trinity: all three members are mentioned— Father, Son, Holy Spirit—as well as the fact that they are equal and they are active together.

2. Some basic principles we wrote down were:

promises:

God will supply our needs according to HIS riches.

God is working in us to complete our salvation.

God will hear our prayers of petition and thanksgiving.

God is with us.

Every knee will bow before Jesus and every tongue confess his name.

The peace of God will guard our hearts and minds.

commands:

We are to humble ourselves like Christ, who gave up his position of equality with God to die for us.

We are to work out our salvation with fear and trembling.

We should act like children of God.

We are not to be anxious.

We should make our requests known unto God.

truths:

Righteousness comes from God on the basis of faith.

An attitude of generous giving is pleasing to God.

God is the source of salvation.

God has given Christ the name above every name.

God is deserving of glory and honor.

3. The key images of God in these passages were:
- Father - provider and caretaker of His children
- Member of Trinity
- King - he has all riches, he deserves glory and honor, and he accepts sacrifices.

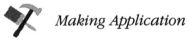 *Making Application*

As you can see from the list above, this study provided many spiritual principles for us to apply to our personal lives. Among the notes we made to ourselves were:

1. Our God is truly an awesome God! We are so rich in Him and in all He provides for us—especially salvation. We need to take full advantage of His riches!

2. When we become anxious and worried, we need to remember again to take our anxieties to God, knowing that He will meet all our needs, according to His riches—which are beyond our comprehension.

3. The passages on bringing glory to God have reminded us that our actions, attitudes, and relationships can bring honor and glory to God.

4. God was pleased with the generous gifts that were sent from Philippi to Paul. Our offerings too are pleasing to him.

Where to Go from Here

Although we exhausted the references in Philippians, we have only scratched the surface of the doctrine of God throughout the Bible. At this point it would be interesting to do a similar study in another book written by Paul, perhaps Galatians or Ephesians, followed by a comparative analysis of both studies. Then material from both books could be combined and examined.

Other topics in Philippians that would be interesting to study are:

Life in Christ

Doctrine of Christ

Prayer

In Closing

It seems as though we have been on a whirlwind tour of the world of computer technology and Bible study methods. Admittedly, our comments have been brief and to the point because the purpose in compiling this book was to encourage you to make additional discoveries and gather more information about computer Bible study. There are many hours, days, and, yes, years of adventures in Bible study ahead of you. God's Word is a treasure trove of immense wealth—we hope you will enjoy using the computer to help you mine those riches!

Bible Software Reference

Computerized Bible/Bible Concordance Programs

IBM-PC or Compatible; MS/PC-DOS.

ASK GOD
Integrated Systems and Information
10316 NE 113th Place
Kirkland WA 98033

(206) 827-3705
(206) 828-6347 FAX

System requirements: IBM-PC or compatible.
Bible versions available: KJV or NIV.
Bible resources available: Bible versions only.
Special program features: Unique artificial intelligence question and answer approach to doing Bible queries.
Comments: This program offers an interesting approach to Bible searches, as it allows the user to search by asking questions. For instance, instead of searching for Noah the user simply types in the question "Who was Noah?" or, in another instance, "Who was Stephen?" and a list of relevant verses appears on the screen. Other questions might include "Where is Jerusalem?" or "What did Jesus teach?" While the program only provides a list of verses in response to the questions rather than actually answering the questions, it does provide a friendly approach to searching the Bible.

BIBLE LINK
Eagle Computing
P.O. Box 490 (615) 928-0333
Elizabethton TN 37644 (615) 928-3677 FAX

System requirements: IBM PC or compatible, 512K RAM, Hercules, CGA, EGA, or VGA monitor, hard disk with 19 MB space, Dos 3.0 or higher.
Bible versions available: KJV.
Bible resources available: Greek and Hebrew lexicons.
Special program features: Hypertext links using the Folio Views engine.
Comments: Bible Link is a Bible study program that provides many advanced features, including complete hypertext-based text management, multiple windows, and a built-in word processor. Based on the Folio Views engine, this program has the advantage of having links between related information—there are links between words in the Bible and their lexicon definition, links from a word to all the verses that contain it, links to root and derivative words, and links that the user can create between the text and personal notes. The user can modify existing links and create new ones.

This program also allows the user to open up to twenty windows, which can be resized, repositioned, or made full-screen. In addition, searches can be made using both the English and Greek/Hebrew words. Finally, verses or definitions that are cut from the program and pasted into the notepad retain their original links. The entire program runs under DOS.

BIBLE MASTER
American Bible Sales
870 S. Anaheim Boulevard (714) 535-4641
Anaheim CA 92805 (800) 535-5131

System requirements: IBM PC or compatible, 384K RAM (640K required for Greek and Hebrew), 3 MB disk space, monochrome or color graphics card. Macintosh version also available.
Bible versions available: KJV, NASB, La Biblia de Las Americas.
Bible resources available: Hebrew/Greek Dictionaries, NASB cross-references and marginal notes, topical studies.
Special program features: Memory resident program allows the user to import (transfer) Bible text from BIBLE MASTER while working in the word processor.
Comments: This is a full-featured computerized Bible program that offers powerful search features, the ability to attach notes to a verse or

word, the ability to display parallel verses, and the option to attach notes to words in the Greek/Hebrew dictionary. It also provides facilities for maintaining separate cross-reference files and for creating a list of topical references.

BIBLE SOURCE
Zondervan Electronic Publishing
5300 Patterson Avenue SE   (800) 727-7759
Grand Rapids MI 49530   (616) 698-6900

System requirements: IBM PC or compatible with hard drive, 640K RAM, DOS 3.2 or later.
Bible versions available: NIV, KJV, NASB .
Bible resources available: *The NIV Exhaustive Concordance*, *The NIV Study Bible Notes*, *The NIV Bible Dictionary*, *An Encyclopedia of Bible Difficulties*, Greek New Testament.
Special program features: *The Analytical NIV Concordance*, including both Goodrick/Kohlenberger numbers and Strong's numbers.
Comments: This Bible study software program is available in individual modules, including Bible translations, original language texts, and related resources that work either separately or together. Special features of the BIBLE SOURCE program include pull-down menus with multiple onscreen windows, extensive mouse support, the ability to display parallel passages and text, speedy searches, and the ability to create Bible studies or outlines using the built-in word processor.

BIBLE WORD PLUS
Hermenutika Computer Bible Research Software
Dept. CBRSBK   (206) 824-3927
P.O. Box 98563   (206) 824-9673 - orders
Seattle WA 98198-0563   (206) 824-7160 FAX

System requirements: DOS 2.1 or higher, any graphics card, 450K RAM, 3-4 MB disk space per Bible text version, mouse optional.
Bible versions available: KJV (with Apocrypha), RSV (with Apocrypha), NIV, UBS 3rd/Nestle-Aland 26th *Greek New Testament*, *Biblica Hebraica Stuttgartensi* Hebrew Old Testament, Rahlf's *Septuaginta* Greek Old Testament.
Bible resources available: Bible texts.
Special program features: Full accented Greek onscreen, pointed and cantillated Hebrew onscreen, results saved to a DOS ASCII file, Pop Up utility lets the program run from within a word processor (uses 4 KB RAM memory). The Pop Up utility also allows the user to export Greek and

Hebrew text into a few multilingual word processors such as Multilingual Scholar and ChiWriter. Features versatile searching capabilities using its REGEX facility. Tutorial manual is included. Works with Gramcord Greek New Testament.

Comments: This is a DOS Bible study software package that features not only English texts, but the Greek Old and New Testaments and the Hebrew Old Testament. It features multiple windows (up to twelve), that can be scrolled through, synchronized, and activated with a mouse. The TSR Pop Up feature lets the user either operate BIBLE WORD PLUS from within a word processor or save the results of a search to a DOS ASCII file. The program is also designed to do original language searches.

EVERYWORD GOOD NEWS BIBLE
American Bible Society
1865 Broadway
New York NY 10023   (212) 581-7400

System requirements: IBM-PC or compatible, 640K RAM, color or monochrome monitor/video card, DOS 3.0 or later.
Bible versions available: Good News Bible.
Bible resources available: WordPerfect Jr.
Special program features: User commenting.
Comments: Offering a range of useful resources for Bible students, this program enables the user to locate references by word or verse, to display text or move through it rapidly, and to save text and materials to a clipboard for further operations or integration with other documents. The WordPerfect Jr. feature provides fully-featured word processing, and a WordPerfect shell allows for transfers between the Bible program and the word processor. The User Commenting feature allows personal notations to be attached to a passage of text.

GODSPEED
Kingdom Age Software
3368 Governor Drive, Suite F-197
San Diego CA 92122   (619) 586-1082

System requirements: IBM-PC or compatible computers, 384K RAM, DOS 2.1 or later, one floppy and one hard disk with 5.66 megabytes of hard disk space.
Bible versions available: KJV, *Nave's Topical Bible*.
Bible resources available: Hebrew and Greek dictionaries.
Special program features: Spell checker for search facility and cross-references.

Comment: It provides over 200,000 cross-references between the Bible text and other resources, and a spell-checker for the search facility suggests related words for search terms that are misspelled.

HOLY BIBLE

Window Book	(800) 524-0380
61 Howard Street	(617) 661-9515
Cambridge MA 02139	(617) 354-3961 FAX

System requirements: 128K RAM, 6 MB of hard disk space for the complete Bible, 900K for Gospels only.
Bible versions available: KJV.
Bible resources available: Bible text only.
Special program features: Hypertext features, topical indexes, full text search, cut and paste.
Comments: This complete Bible on disk features hypertext search and retrieval features. The program comes in two versions, either the Complete Bible or the Complete Gospels. Each contains the complete text, together with topical indexes, a table of contents, full text searching, and cut-and-paste features.

HOLY SCRIPTURES

Christian Technologies	
P.O. Box 2201	(800) 366-8320
Independence MO 64055	(816) 478-8320

System requirements: IBM-PC or compatible, 384K RAM, DOS 2.11 or higher, hard disk.
Bible versions available: KJV, ASV, RSV (with Apocrypha), NRSV (with Apocrypha), NIV, New American Bible with Revised New Testament (Catholic), The Living Bible, Reina Valera (Spanish).
Resources available: Greek and Hebrew transliteration and definitions.
Special features: Wide choice of translations.
Comments: This program provides a DOS (or Windows) compatible Bible study program that offers a wide range of translations and basic Bible software features.

ONLINE BIBLE

Online Bible	
P.O. Box 21	(800) 243-7124
Bronson MI 49028	(517) 369-6035

System requirements: IBM-PC or compatible.

Bible versions available: KJV, NIV, RSV, Greek and Hebrew texts.
Bible resources available: *The Treasury of Scripture Knowledge*, King James lexicon.
Special program features: Also available with other resources on a CD-ROM disk.
Comments: This is a low-cost, full-featured, and comprehensive Bible study package. Study features include displaying verses, doing searches, and creating topic and verse lists. There is a built-in text editor as well as a Notes facility that allows text to be linked to specific verses in the Bible. A version of the ONLINE BIBLE is included in a new CD-ROM product called "The Holy Bible and Other Christian Shareware."

PC STUDY BIBLE
Biblesoft   (800) 995-9058
22014 Seventh Avenue S. #201   (206) 824-0862
Seattle WA 98198   (206) 824-1828 FAX

System requirements: IBM PC or compatible
Bible versions available: KJV, NIV, ASV, RSV, NKJV, and *The Living Bible.*
Bible resources available: *Exhaustive Concordance, Nave's Topical Bible, Nelson's Bible Dictionary, Strong's Dictionary, Englishman's Concordance, Vine's Expository Dictionary of Biblical Words,* and *The Treasury of Scripture Knowledge.*
Special program features: Completely integrated Bible translations and resources. Three editions available: NIV or KJV Edition (includes *Nave's Topical Bible*); Master Edition (includes *NIV, KJV, Nave's Topical Bible* and *Nelson's Bible Dictionary*); Reference Library (includes *KJV, NIV, Nave's Topical Bible, Nelson's Bible Dictionary, Strong's Dictionary, Englishman's Concordance,* and *Vine's Expository Dictionary of Biblcial Words*). All editions feature Exhaustive Concordance and the integrated word processor - Notepad.
Comment: A new interface allows for multiple, overlapping windows on the screen so that the user can access several translations and resources at once. The program provides the standard electronic Bible features including searching and finding verses, comparing different translations, and creating study notes. With the extensive cross-reference capability the user can move between related verses and access related portions of reference works. Windows version available.

QUICK VERSE
Parsons Technology
P.O. Box 100   (800) 223-6925
Hiawatha IA 52233-0100   (319) 395-9626

System requirements: IBM-PC or compatible, 512K RAM, 2.5 MB hard disk space for each Bible version, and 4 MB for Greek and Hebrew versions.

Bible versions available: KJV, NKJV, NIV, RSV, NRSV, The Living Bible, Hebrew and Greek Transliterated Bibles.

Bible resources available: *Nave's Topical Bible* .

Special program features: Fast searches, ability to create topical indexes, multiple onscreen windows.

Comment: Provides a low-cost, yet easily accessible and usable approach to Bible computing. The DOS version is a multifeatured Bible system that provides a full range of Bible texts (including KJV, NIV, The Living Bible, and NCV). The program offers search features including words, phrases, partial words, Boolean operators, and wildcards. Multiple windows are supported, and a footnoting feature allows notes to be tagged to words and verses. Topical indexes are supported, and original word definitions are provided with the Greek and Hebrew transliterated Bible add-on.

SEEDMASTER
White Harvest Software
P.O. Box 97153   (919) 870-0775 Voice & FAX
Raleigh NC 27624-7153   (919) 846-2141 Bulletin Board

System requirements: IBM-PC or compatible, DOS 2.1 or higher, 512K RAM, and 4.5 MB hard disk space (Microsoft Windows 3.1 or higher).

Bible versions available: KJV, NIV, RVA Spanish, UBS Greek New Testament.

Bible resources available: Primary versions and program features.

Special program features: Commentary, Boolean operators, multiple windows on the screen, Boolean searching and search statistics, friendly user interface, Rabbit Trail Support, Interlinear Bible, Associator, Greek/Spanish support.

Comments: SEEDMASTER is a comprehensive program that is available in both DOS and Windows versions. It includes multiple windows (up to three on a screen), a menu-driven Bible book selection, a Commentary feature that allows the user to enter and recall comments for a certain verse, and complete searching facilities including wildcards and Boolean operators. Other features include over half a million cross-references, Greek and Hebrew lexicons, and fast searches.

Other features include Rabbit Trail Support, which lets the user pursue study and search ideas, move between modes, and track previous searches and results. The program provides search statistics, and the Associator approximates what words in one version are associated with those in another (such as KJV versus the Greek New Testament). It is possible to view interlinear Bible versions, which means that different translations are located in the same window instead of in separate ones. Greek is represented either in transliterated or approximated form. (The latter is a combination of ASCII Greek symbols together with substitutes for the others.) Spanish is displayed with accented letters.

THE WORD ADVANCED STUDY SYSTEM
Wordsoft/Word Inc.
5221 North O'Connor Blvd., Suite 1000   (214) 401-2344 FAX
Irving TX 75039   (214) 556-1900

System requirements: IBM-PC or compatible, DOS 3.0 or later, 3.2 MB hard disk space for program and temporary files, and 2.6 MB for each Bible version. Greek New Testament requires 4.2 MB, Strong's *Dictionary* 4.4 MB, and Hebrew Old Testament 9 MB disk space.

Bible versions available: KJV, NKJV, NRSV, Hebrew Old Testament, Greek New Testament.

Bible resources available: *Strong's Concordance/Dictionary.*

Special program features: Graphical user interface that does not require Microsoft Windows, advanced tools for Greek and Hebrew language analysis.

Comments: This is a graphical, windows-oriented program that does not require Microsoft Windows. It features an intuitive, easy-to-use graphical interface that is ideal for both beginning and advanced users. Parallel versions can be viewed in multiple windows, and the windows can be moved, resized, and iconified. Advanced features such as lexical and grammatical analysis are included as well as fully-formed Greek and Hebrew characters. Windows can be linked together to display the same verse in various translations or languages.

With this program it is possible to attach notes to verses, create indexes of verses, and use a built-in multilingual (Hebrew, Greek, English) text editor. The program works with either keyboard or mouse.

THE WORD PROCESSOR
Bible Research Systems
2013 Wells Branch Parkway #304   (800) 423-1228
Austin TX 78728   (512) 251-7541

System requirements: IBM-PC or compatible, color or monochrome video card and monitor, mouse optional, 640K RAM, DOS 3.0 or higher, hard disk.

Bible versions available: KJV, NKJV, NIV, RSV.

Bible resources available: Strong's *Concordance*.

Special program features: Librarian, Personal Commentary, Chain Reference, Topics, People, Chronological Bible, Verse Typist.

Comments: This a complete library of Bible tools and resources for both basic and advanced Bible study. Running under DOS (for IBM-PC and compatible), with a Windows version also available, it provides access to Bible texts and a full range of standard search and retrieval features. It also offers a choice of add-on packages that are designed for more specialized and advanced purposes.

The program offers a number of English translations, together with access to Strong's numbers and the definitions and meanings of the underlying Greek and Hebrew words (for the King James Version). The program provides searches on words or phrases, including partial word lookup and complex searches. Multiple synchronized windows are supported for viewing multiple translations.

One add-on package is the Librarian, which allows the user to save lists of references that can then be edited, merged, sorted, or combined. The program also includes Bible Topics and People reference lists, a Personal Commentary that allows notes to be added to each verse, a Chain Reference feature, and a Chronological Bible that groups verses in an organized fashion and provides chronological charts and outlines. The Verse Typist makes it possible to use the Word Processor program from within a standard word processing program. The Word Processor is a complete set of tools for studying the Bible. Its extensive list of add-ons include support for topical and chronological studies of the Scriptures, as well as studies of geography and biblical words.

WORDSEARCH

Navpress Software	(800) 366-7788
P.O. Box 35006	(719) 260-0404
Colorado Springs CO 80935	(719) 598-0749 FAX

System requirements: IBM-PC or compatible, hard disk (2.7 MB per translation), 512K RAM, floppy disk drive, DOS 2.0 or above.

Bible versions available: KJV, NKJV, NIV, NRSV, New American Bible, The Living Bible.

Bible resources available: *Strong's Ties to the Greek and Hebrew*, and also *Nave's Topics* add-on packages.

Special features: Great flexibility in refining searches, fast searches.

Comments: This Bible study package is designed to be both highly interactive and capable of fast searches. Features include split screens for viewing multiple translations, pull-down menus, a window for entering personal comments on a verse, a notepad for creating study notes and ideas, context-sensitive help, and fast searches (usually two seconds or less).

Windows Bible Study Software

BIBLE WINDOWS
Silver Mountain Software
1029 Tanglewood
Cedar Hill TX 75014 (214) 293-2920

System requirements: IBM-PC or compatible, Microsoft Windows.
Bible versions available: KJV, RSV with Apocrypha, tagged Greek Testament, tagged Hebrew Old Testament (BHS), Septuagint, Latin Vulgate.
Bible resources included: Greek Dictionary, Hebrew Dictionary.
Special features: Interlinear display, onscreen description of all grammatical tags, synchronized windows, dictionary search of Greek and Hebrew words. Fonts include Greek, Hebrew, Coptic, and Latin.
Comments: A Windows-based package, this program's strength is grammatical search features for Greek and Hebrew. Aside from English translations, it provides the Greek New Testament with complete grammatical tags and dictionary forms, together with a comprehensive Greek Dictionary. The same is provided for the BHS Hebrew text and the Septuagint (Greek Old Testament).

Other features include the ability to display onscreen descriptions of Greek and Hebrew words, to do fast grammatical searches, to look up Greek and Hebrew words easily, and also to do Interlinear Display, which allows for analysis while viewing the text. Text can be copied to a built-in clipboard, and verses can be inserted into Windows word processor files. Extensive online help is available.

BIBLEWORKS FOR WINDOWS
Hermenutika Computer Bible Research Software
Dept. CBRSBK (206) 824-3927
P.O. Box 98563 (206) 824-9673 - orders
Seattle WA 98198-0563 (206) 824-7160 FAX

System requirements: IBM-PC or compatible, Microsoft 3.1 or higher, 4 MB RAM minimum, 5 MB hard disk space per text. VGA monitor is recommended, as well as 386 SX or higher processor.
Bible versions available: KJV (linked to resources profiled below), RSV (with Apocrypha), ASV (1901), UBS 3rd/Nestle-Aland 26th *Greek New Testament*, *Biblica Hebraica Stuttgartensia* Hebrew Old Testament, Rahlf's *Septuagint* Greek Old Testament, and Latin Vulgate.

Bible resources available: Strong's *Concordance*, Englishman's *Concordance*, 100,000 Greek and Hebrew words with verb parsings (including tense, voice, mood), Greek and Hebrew words linked to corrected Strong's numbers, Thayer's *Greek Lexicon*, Brown-Driver Briggs *Hebrew Lexicon*, (both lexicons are linked to corrected Strong's numbers), *The Treasury of Scripture Knowledge.* TSK has cross-references and a commentary.
Special program features: Advanced features for study of Greek and Hebrew words and texts.

Comments: This comprehensive Windows software program provides many advanced features including extensive lists of available Bible translations, Greek/Hebrew texts, and computerized resources. The program is designed to provide fast searches (from simple word searches, to wildcards, multiple word, Boolean, proximity, and exact phrase searches) in English as well as in Greek and Hebrew. Grammatical searches can also be done.

The Greek and Hebrew Bible texts (Greek NT, Hebrew OT, and LXX Greek OT) are fully grammatically analyzed, providing information on parsing and lexical forms. Even without a knowledge of Greek or Hebrew, the Strong's numbers and electronic lexicons can be used to look up words and definitions.

For multilingual word processing, the program features a Multi Document Interface (MDI) editor that supports Greek, Hebrew, and English including automatic right-to-left typing of Hebrew. From this editor it is possible to cut and paste to other Windows word processors. Fully scalable True Type and Postscript Type 1 Biblical Greek and Hebrew fonts are included in the package with full diacritics and pointing.

The program is sold in bundle configurations, depending on whether the emphasis and interest is on studying Bible translations or working with Greek and Hebrew texts and languages.

LOGOS BIBLE SOFTWARE	(800) 87-LOGOS Toll Free Orders
Logos Research Systems	(206) 679-6575 Main Line
2117 200th Avenue West	(206) 679-4496 Technical Support
Oak Harbor WA 98277-4049	(206) 675-8169 FAX

System requirements: IBM-PC or compatible, Microsoft Windows, hard disk.
Bible versions available: KJV, NKJV, NIV, RSV, NRSV, ASV 1901, Greek texts (Byzantine/Majority Textform), Nestle-Aland 26th/UBS 3rd, *Textus Receptus* (Stephen's 1550), *Textus Receptus* (Scrivener's 1891), Hebrew texts (*Biblia Hebraica Stuttgartensia*), RVA Spanish.
Bible resources available: *The Treasury of Scripture Knowledge, Strong's Lexicon,* TVM (Tense Voice Mood), *Nave's Topical Bible.*
Special program features: One of the largest selections of add-on Bible versions and resources available.

Comments: This Bible-based software system offers an impressive array of Bible versions and add-ons and has many features that make it ideal for intermediate and advanced users. The program runs under Microsoft Windows and has as one of its strengths a graphical, visual approach to Bible study computing, with pull-down menus, button bars, and multiple windows. The software offers efficient searches using English, Greek, and Hebrew, and allows for more complex searches using AND and OR. Other features include notepads and verse notes, cross-references to *The Treasury of Scripture Knowledge*, multiple windows, and different onscreen fonts. Users can create topical indexes of verses and use the Tense Voice Mood module to parse any Greek or Hebrew word.

PC STUDY BIBLE FOR WINDOWS

Biblesoft   (800) 995-9058
22014 Seventh Avenue S. #201   (206) 824-0862
Seattle WA 98198   (206) 824-1828 FAX

System requirements: Windows 3.1
Bible versions available: *KJV, NIV, ASV, RSV, NKJV*, and *The Living Bible*.
Bible resources available: *Exhaustive Concordance, Nave's Topical Bible, Nelson's Bible Dictionary, Strong's Dictionary, Englishman's Concordance, Vine's Expository Dictionary of Biblical Words*, and *The Treasury of Scripture Knowledge*.
Special program features: Completely integrated Bible translations and resources. Three editions available: *NIV* or *KJV* Edition (includes *Nave's Topical Bible*); Master Edition (includes *NIV, KJV, Nave's Topical Bible* and *Nelson's Bible Dictionary*); Reference Library (includes *KJV, NIV, Nave's Tropical Bible, Nelson's Bible Dictionary, Strong's Dictionary, Englishman's Concordance*, and *Vine's Expository Dictionary of Biblical Words*).
Comment: A new Windows interface/desktop features new icon toolbars, mouse shortcuts, and resizeable windows, for organization and access. Cross-referencing and unlimited windows let the user access information from any resource at any time. Easy data transfer to Windows word processors or desktop publishers using Biblesoft's new Appendable Clipboard. Complete online Help System for clear, easy-to-understand instructions on program use.

QUICK VERSE FOR WINDOWS

Parsons Technology
P.O. Box 100   (800) 223-6925
Hiawatha IA 52233-0100   (319) 395-9626

System requirements: IBM-PC or compatible, hard disk, Microsoft Windows 3.0 or later, mouse recommended, and printer optional.
Bible versions available: KJV, NKJV, NIV, RSV, NRSV, The Living Bible, Hebrew and Greek Transliterated Bibles.
Special program features: *Nave's Topical Bible*, the ability to change fonts and type, unlimited number of windows.
Comments: This Windows-based Bible program is easy to use and, yet, it provides the ability to work with different Bible versions using multiple windows, to do speedy searches through its Quick Search feature, to cut and paste verses from the clipboard to personal notes, and to transfer Bible text to a word processor.

SEEDMASTER (see listing under IBM-PC and Compatible)

THOMPSON CHAIN HYPERBIBLE
Kirkbride Technology   (800) 428-4385
P.O. Box 606   (317) 633-1900
Indianapolis IN 46206-0606   (317) 633-1444 FAX

System requirements: 80386 or higher processor, one floppy disk drive, DOS 3.1 or higher, Microsoft Windows 3.0 or higher, VGA graphics, mouse, 4 MB RAM, 16 MB hard disk space.
Bible versions available: KJV and NIV in parallel.
Bible resources available: *Thompson Chain Reference Bible,* electronic concordance, Bible atlases, topical searches, character outlines, outline studies of each book.
Special program features: Thompson chain reference system, extensive listing of resources.
Comments: This is a computerized version of the *Thompson Chain Reference Bible* with the text of the KJV and the NIV. The program displays multiple translations side-by-side, has an AutoRead function that lets the user read the text at different speeds (200-1000 words per minute), and has a Placemark feature.

Other features of the program include word and phrase searches, an electronic concordance (for both translations), an extensive help system, support for topical studies through topical searches as well as a list of preselected topics (with subtopics and pilot numbers), a Bible atlas, links to Windows word processor, biblical character studies, archaeological studies, book outlines, Bible memorization mnemonics, location finders, festivals, and listings of places of worship.

The entire program runs under Microsoft Windows, so it takes advantage of the Windows interface, supporting icons, pull-down menus, and extensive use of the mouse.

Greek and Hebrew Resources

BIBLE WINDOWS (see listing under Windows Bible Study Software)

BIBLE WORD PLUS (see listing under IBM-PC or Compatible)

BIBLEWORKS FOR WINDOWS (see listing under Windows Bible Study Software)

GRAMCORD, GRAMSEARCH, GRAMGREEK
Gramcord Institute
2218 NE Brookview Drive   (206) 576-3000
Vancouver WA 98686   (503) 761-0626 FAX

System requirements: IBM-PC or compatible.
Comments: An integrated concordance/study system that emphasizes tools for studying Old and New Testament words. Includes facilities for working with grammatical constructions and advanced searches. The Gramcord Institute publishes a wide range of Greek/Hebrew study tools, including GRAMSEARCH, GRAMGREEK, and PARSER PLUS. (Details are provided in chapter 4, "Parsing with Programs.")

GREEK TOOLS
Parsons Technology
P.O. Box 100   (800) 223-6925
Hiawatha IA 52233-0100   (319) 395-9626

System requirements: IBM-PC or compatible, 512K RAM, DOS 2.11 or higher, floppy or hard disk, graphics card. Printer optional.
Special program features: Greek lexicon database, grammar guide and reference, manuscript evidences database, textual criticism, multilingual word processor.
Comments: This program provides electronic tools to study Greek words and grammar. Unique features include the ability to access information in original Greek manuscripts and to do textual criticism.

HAMMOREH
Gramcord Institute
2218 NE Brookview Drive   (206) 576-3000
Vancouver WA 98686   (503) 761-0626 FAX

System Requirements: IBM-PC or compatible, VGA color graphics card, 16 MB disk space.

Comments: This is a Hebrew grammar tutorial series that uses color to help teach grammatical forms of the language. Going beyond flashcard approaches, it provides color-coded analyses of Hebrew parts of speech, including strong/weak verbs etc.

HEBREW TOOLS
Parsons Technology
P.O. Box 100   (800) 223-6925
Hiawatha IA 52233-0100   (319) 395-9626

System requirements: IBM-PC or compatible, 512K RAM, DOS 2.11 or higher, floppy or hard disk, graphics card. Printer optional.
Special program features: Hebrew lexicon database, grammar guide and reference, multilingual word processor.
Comments: This complete electronic drill and review program is designed to help you learn biblical Hebrew. It includes Menahem Mansoor's *Biblical Hebrew Step by Step*.

HEBREW WORDMASTER I & II
Davka Corporation
7074 N. Western Avenue   (800) 621-8227
Chicago IL 60645   (312) 465-4070

System requirements: IBM-PC or compatible.
Special program features: Drills, games, and quizzes in Hebrew.
Comments: This educational program provides entertaining ways to learn Hebrew words.

LBASE
Silver Mountain Software
1029 Tanglewood
Cedar Hill TX 75014   (214) 293-2920

System requirements: IBM-PC or compatible.
Comments: This program is designed for grammatical and concordance studies of various texts, including the Greek, Hebrew, *Septuagint* (LXX), and Latin texts.

LEARNING TO READ HEBREW
Davka Corporation
7074 N. Western Avenue   (800) 621-8227
Chicago IL 60645   (312) 465-4070

System requirements: IBM-PC or compatible.
Comments: This program teaches the user how to read Hebrew. It is designed especially for individuals with no previous knowledge of the language or alphabet. This program has fourteen units that cover vowels, letters, and words. A tape is included as well.

MEMCARDS BIBLICAL HEBREW VOCABULARY
MEMCARDS GREEK FORMS AND PARSING
MEMCARDS GREEK VOCABULARY
Memorization Technology
P.O. Box 60788
Palo Alto CA 94306-0788

System requirements: IBM-PC or compatible with 512K RAM, with graphics card. Dot matrix and laser printers supported.
Comments: These programs are language learning helps based on Greek and biblical Hebrew vocabulary words.

WORD ADVANCED STUDY SYSTEM (see listing under IBM-PC or Compatible)

Sermon Software

AUTOILLUSTRATOR
Autoillustrator
P.O. Box 5056
Greeley CO 80632   (303) 330-8768

System requirements: Versions for MS-DOS (DOS 3.1, 640K memory, 2 MB+ hard disk space, optional mouse), 386/486 system (same as above except 4 MB memory needed), and Macintosh (Hypercard 1.2.2 or later, 1 MB disk space or more).
Comments: This is a comprehensive filing and retrieval system for Bible illustration material. It offers search, browse, and editing features, and also different modules for parables/stories, leadership, preaching, and others.

BIBLE ILLUSTRATOR
Parsons Technology
P.O. Box 100   (800) 223-6925
Hiawatha IA 52233-0100   (319) 395-9626

System Requirements: IBM-PC or compatible, 384K RAM, DOS 2.11 or higher, 3 MB hard disk space.

Comments: This program contains 2,500 online illustrations, both from current news headlines and from experiences of pastors. It includes news items, quotes, and anecdotes that are stored in a database, are searchable, and can be printed out.

ILLUSTRATION FINDER
Voicings Publications
P.O. Box 3102   (800) 827-9401
Margate NJ 08402   (609) 822-9401

System requirements: IBM-PC or compatible, 640K RAM, hard disk with 4.5MB disk space.

Comments: This program is designed to store, manage, and retrieve sermon illustrations. It includes editing, printing, and exporting into word processing programs.

INFOSEARCH SERIES:
CURRENT THOUGHTS AND TRENDS
HUMOR COLLECTION
HYMNAL FOR WORSHIP AND CELEBRATION
HOSANNA! MUSIC PRAISE AND WORSHIP
SERMON ILLUSTRATIONS
Navpress Software   (800) 366-7788
P.O. Box 35006   (719) 260-0404
Colorado Springs CO 80935   (719) 598-0749 FAX

System requirements: IBM-PC or compatible, 640K RAM, hard disk, DOS 3.3 or above.

Comments: This is a series of sermon illustrations, research, and music-oriented programs that use the INFOSEARCH filing system to organize and retrieve information. (See further details in the chapter 6, "The Electronic Sermon.")

LESSON MAKER
Navpress Software   (800) 366-7788
P.O. Box 35006   (719) 260-0404
Colorado Springs CO 80935   (719) 598-0749 FAX

System Requirements: IBM-PC or compatible, 640K RAM, hard disk, DOS 3.3 or higher.

Comments: This program is designed to create customized Bible studies designed to suit the particular needs of a group. The program consists of a database of more than 18,000 questions that are accessed by passage or topic selection. These questions can be modified; preorganized studies are also provided. This DOS-based program does not need to be used in conjunction with a Bible software program.

NEW BIBLE LIBRARY (See CD-ROM Software and Resources)

SERMON WARE
Voicings Publications
P.O. Box 3102   (800) 827-9401
Margate NJ 08402   (609) 822-9401

System requirements: IBM-PC or compatible, 640K RAM, hard disk with 4.5MB disk space. Macintosh version.
Comments: This is a series of complete sermons on disk.

Multilingual Software and Resources

CHIWRITER
Horstmann Software
P.O. Box 1807   (408) 298-0828
San Jose CA 95109-1807   (408) 298-6157

System requirements: IBM-PC or compatible, 384K memory, CGA or higher graphics card, two floppy drives or one floppy and one hard disk, dot matrix or laser printer.
Special program features: Multilingual and scientific word processing capabilities.
Comments: CHIWRITER provides multilingual word processing, together with the option of doing scientific word processing. Provides multiple fonts and languages, including Greek and Hebrew. The program is WYSIWYG (What You See Is What You Get). A font designer is also provided, as well as support for a wide range of printers. (See chapter 5 "The Tower of Babel on a Disk," for more details.)

MULTILINGUAL SCHOLAR
Gamma Productions
710 Wilshire Boulevard, Suite 609   (310) 394-8622
Santa Monica CA 90401   (310) 395-4214 FAX

System requirements: IBM-PC or compatible, 512K RAM, hard disk recommended.

Special program features: A wide range of languages is supported.
Comments: Together with word processing features, this program offers a wide range of languages including Greek and Hebrew.

PC HEBREW WRITER
Davka Corporation
7074 N. Western Avenue   (800) 621-8227
Chicago IL 60645   (312) 465-4070

System requirements: IBM-PC or compatible.
Special program features: Hebrew and English word processing.
Comments: This Hebrew and English word processor includes a range of standard word processing features.

SCRIPTURE FONTS
Zondervan Electronic Publishing
5300 Patterson Avenue SE   (800) 727-7759
Grand Rapids MI 49530   (616) 698-6900

System requirements: IBM-PC or compatible.
Comments: This program makes it possible to use Greek and Hebrew from within WordPerfect 5.0 or 5.1

UNIVERSE FOR WINDOWS
Gamma Productions
710 Wilshire Boulevard, Suite 609   (310) 394-8622
Santa Monica CA 90401   (310) 395-4214 FAX

System requirements: IBM-PC or compatible, Windows 3.1 or later, EGA or better graphics card/monitor, Windows 3.1 supported printer, mouse recommended.
Special program features: Windows features, wide range of languages and fonts, foreign spell checking, alternate keyboard mappings (arrangements).
Comments: This Windows multilingual word processor allows easy WYSIWYG creation of foreign words and dozens of supported languages from around the world. It provides spell checking in foreign languages, and the LanguageLink feature makes it possible to use certain languages in other Windows applications.

WORDPERFECT HEBREW
Davka Corporation
7074 N. Western Avenue   (800) 621-8227
Chicago IL 60645   (312) 465-4070

System requirements: IBM-PC or compatible.
Comments: With this program it is possible to work with Hebrew from within WordPerfect 5.1. The user can create documents in Hebrew alone, or in conjunction with English.

WORDSEARCH BRIDGE

Navpress Software	(800) 366-7788
P.O. Box 35006	(719) 260-0404
Colorado Springs CO 80935	(719) 598-0749 FAX

System requirements: IBM-PC or compatible, 640K memory, 5.25 or 3.5 inch floppy disk drive, DOS 2.0 or above.
Comments: This program is designed to allow access to NavPress Software, WORDsearch, INFOsearch, Strong's, or other programs from within a word processor.

CD-ROM Software and Resources

ABS REFERENCE BIBLE ON CD-ROM
American Bible Society
1865 Broadway
New York NY 10023   (212) 581-7400

System Requirements: IBM-PC or compatible, CD-ROM drive and associated software.
Bible versions available: KJV, NKJV, RSV, NRSV, NASV, Today's English Bible, Spanish Bible (RVA), German Bible (Luther), BHS Hebrew Old Testament, UBS 3rd Greek Old Testament, Rahlf's *Septuagint*, Latin Vulgate, English translation of the *Septuagint*.
Bible resources available: *Hebrew Harmony of the Gospels*, *Greek Harmony of the Gospels*, *English Harmony of the Gospels*, other Harmonies, *Apostolic Fathers* in English, *Works of Josephus*, *Dictionary of Bible and Religion*.
Comments: A complete reference library of Bible versions and resources on CD-ROM.

ATLA RELIGION DATABASE
American Theological Library Association
820 Church Street
Evanston IL 60201   (708) 869-7788

System requirements: Priced for professional use, so you are advised to use it at a library or seminary.

Comments: ATLA Religion Database offers in-depth, scholarly information on religion.

THE BIBLE LIBRARY
THE NEW BIBLE LIBRARY

Ellis Enterprises   (800) 729-9500
4205 McAuley Blvd., Suite 385   (405) 749-0273
Oklahoma City OK 73120   (405) 751-5168 FAX

System requirements: IBM-PC or compatible, DOS 5.0 or higher, 640 KB RAM, CGA or higher graphics card, hard disk with 1 MB or more of space, CD-ROM drive and associated programs, and mouse.

Bible versions available: ASV, Chronological Bible (KJV), KJV, Literal English Translation with Strong's Numbers, *The Living Bible, MicroBible, New American Bible with Revised New Testament,* NASB, NIV, *New Jerusalem Version,* NKJV, RVA (Spanish), RSV, *Simple English Bible* (New Testament), *Transliterated Bible,* and *Transliterated Pronounceable Bible.*

Bible resources available: Harris's *Theological Wordbook of the Old Testament,* Strong's *Greek and Hebrew Dictionary, Vine's Expository Dictionary of Old and New Testament Words, Barclay's Daily Bible Study Series,* Gray's *Bible Study Notes,* Matthew Henry's *Concise Commentary of the Whole Bible,* Morris's *Introduction to the Books of the Bible,* the *Complete Works of Josephus,* Easton's *Bible Dictionary,* Edersheim's *Life and Times of Jesus,* Elwell's *Evangelical Dictionary of Theology,* 2,500 Sermon Outlines, 500 Gospel Sermon Illustrations, 101 Hymn Stories, 12 Bible Maps.

Comments: This comprehensive Bible study resource package is a revised version of the BIBLE LIBRARY, which was previously developed by Ellis Enterprises. It features a wide range of Bibles and biblical resources and IBM's SoftCopy Navigator software to help the user work with and manage the information.

CD WORD LIBRARY

Logos Research Systems   (800) 87-LOGOS Toll Free Orders
2117 200th Avenue West   (206) 679-6575 Main Line
Oak Harbor WA 98277-4049   (206) 679-4496 Technical Support
                                         (206) 675-8169 FAX

System requirements: IBM-PC or compatible, 80286 or higher microprocessor, 10 MB hard disk space, Hercules or EGA/VGA graphics board, MS-DOS 3.0 or higher, Microsoft Windows, CD-ROM drive with MSCDEX 2.0 or higher.

Bible versions available: KJV, NIV, NASV, RSV, Greek New Testament, and *Septuagint.*

Bible resources available: Three Greek Lexicons, including Bauer Arndt Gingrich (BAG), Intermediate Liddell and Scott lexicon, *Theogical Dictionary of the New Testament, New Bible Dictionary, Harper's Bible Dictionary, Harper's Bible Commentary, Bible Knowledge Commentary, Jerome Bible Commentary.*

Comments: A comprehensive CD-ROM library with an emphasis on Greek study references. Developed in conjunction with the Dallas Theological Seminary, it uses hypertext technology to allow the user to interact more efficiently with the texts and Bible resources.

MASTER SEARCH BIBLE
Tri Star Publishing
275 Gibraltar Road   (800) 292-4253
Horsham PA 19044   (215) 441-6451

System requirements: IBM-PC or compatible, 640 K memory, MS-DOS 2.0 or higher, 20MB hard disk, CD-ROM drive, printer.

Bible versions available: KJV, NASV, NIV.

Bible resources available: *Strong's Concordance*, NIV Study Bible, NIV Scofield Study Bible, *Wycliffe Bible Encyclopedia, Handbook to Bible Study, Expository Dictionary of Bible Words, New Manners and Customs of Bible Times, Wycliff Historical Geography of Bible Lands,* and *New International Dictionary of Biblical Archaeology.*

Comments: This program provides a wealth of valuable Bibles and resources, including some that are not available through other CD-ROM or online Bible programs.

Telecommunications Services

ATLA RELIGION DATABASE:
RELIGION INDEX ONE
RELIGION INDEX TWO
INDEX TO BOOK REVIEWS IN RELIGION
RESEARCH IN MINISTRY
METHODIST REVIEW INDEX

Vendor:
Dialog Information Services
3460 Hillview Avenue   (800) 3-DIALOG
Palo Alto CA 94304   (415) 858-2700

Producer:
American Theological Library Association
820 Church Street
Evanston IL 60201   (708) 869-7788

System requirements: Personal computer or terminal, modem, communications software, telephone line.
Comments: Provides detailed, scholarly information on religion from a variety of religion databases.

CATHOLIC NEWS SERVICE
CATHOLIC TRENDS
CHURCH NEWS INTERNATIONAL
LUTHERAN NEWS SERVICE
RNS DAILY NEWS REPORTS
UNITED METHODIST INFORMATION SERVICE
Newsnet
945 Haverford Road   (800) 345-1301
Bryn Mawr PA 19010   (215) 527-8030

System requirements: Personal computer or terminal, modem, communications software, telephone line.
Comments: This services provides electronic newsletters on a variety of religious subjects. Each service differs in content, orientation, and price.

ECUNET
Online Services Corporation
P.O. Box 246
Canton CT 06019-0246   (800) 733-2863

System requirements: IBM-PC or compatible, or terminal, and modem/communications software.
Comments: A communications and exchange facility for different religious denominations.

Games and Recreational Software

BIBLE ADVENTURES
Wisdom Tree Software   (800) 77-BIBLE
2700 E. Imperial Highway, Bldg. A   (714) 528-3456
Brea CA 92621   (714) 961-1890

System Requirements: IBM-PC or compatible.
Comments: Old Testament story adventures.

BIBLE BUILDER
Everbright Software
P.O. Box 8020
Redwood City CA 94063   (415) 368-3200

System requirements: IBM-PC or compatible, EGA or VGA video card
and monitor, 640K RAM, DOS 2.1 or higher (sound card, mouse, and hard
disk are optional).
Bible versions available: KJV, NIV, RSV, The Living Bible.
Comments: A combination of education and entertainment, this programs tests Bible knowledge through action adventure games.

BIBLE CRYPTOQUOTES
Sunburst Software
37838 Sweetbrush Street
Palmdale CA 93552   (805) 267-6744

System requirements: IBM-PC or compatible.
Comments: This game is designed to increase Bible knowledge through
the challenge of unraveling codes to secret verses.

BIBLE PAINT AND LEARN
Ark Multimedia Publishing
3323 W. Mercury Blvd.
Hampton VA 23666   (804) 838-9270

System requirements: IBM-PC or compatible.
Comments: This is a Bible painting and educational program.

BIBLE TIME FUN
Whiz Kid Productions
10809 Poplar Street
Loma Linda CA 92354

System Requirements: IBM-PC or compatible.
Comments: This is a collection of Bible games that are not only
entertaining but educational.

COMPUTER BIBLE STORIES
Timed-Sequence Learning
316 Townes Drive
Nashville TN 37211   (615) 331-7107

System requirements: IBM-PC or compatible, 640K RAM, VGA or MCGA graphics card.
Comments: Realistic depictions of Bible stories, including text, pictures, and music.

DEFENDER OF THE FAITH

Navpress Software	(800) 366-7788
P.O. Box 35006	(719) 260-0404
Colorado Springs CO 80935	(719) 598-0749 FAX

System requirements: IBM-PC or compatible.
Comments: This adventure game is based on the life and times of David.

EXODUS

Wisdom Tree Software	(800) 77-BIBLE
2700 E. Imperial Highway, Bldg. A	(714) 528-3456
Brea CA 92621	

System requirements: IBM-PC or compatible.
Comments: This game focuses on Israel's Exodus out of Egypt.

GERASENE DEMONIAC
American Bible Society
1865 Broadway
New York NY 10023   (212) 581-7400

System requirements: IBM-PC or compatible, floppy and hard disk, laserdisc player, sound card, graphics card.
Comments: A multimedia experience of the story of the Gerasene demoniac.

GUIDED PRAYER JOURNAL
Christian Growth Software
211 N. 89th
Wauwatosa WI 53226

System requirements: IBM-PC or compatible.
Comments: This is a prayer-list management system.

HEARTWARMERS FOR WINDOWS
Softhoughts
4625 San Felipe Suite 1100
Houston TX 77027   (800) 388-4775

System requirements: IBM-PC or compatible, Microsoft Windows.
Comments: This program displays inspirational and motivational thoughts for each day of the year.

IN HIS TIME
Colonnade Technologies   (800) 848-5480
11820 Northrup Way, Suite 200   (206) 869-8838
Bellevue WA 98005   (206) 827-0646 FAX

System requirements: IBM-PC or compatible, Microsoft Windows.
Comments: This is a graphical, Windows-based personal information manager with a religious emphasis.

JOURNEY TO THE PROMISED LAND
Ark Multimedia Publishing
3323 W. Mercury Blvd.
Hampton VA 23666   (804) 838-2807

System requirements: IBM-PC or compatible.
Comments: An adventure game based on the Israelites' journey to Canaan.

MULTIMEDIA FAMILY BIBLE
Candlelight Publishing
1136 East Harmony Avenue, Suite 204   (800) 677-3045
Mesa AZ 84204-5844   (602) 545-6707

System requirements: IBM-PC/XT/286/386/486, DOS 3.0 or higher, VGA graphics card, 512K RAM, 11 MB disk space, mouse and sound board optional.
Bible versions available: KJV.
Special program features: Multimedia effects, including digitized Bible paintings, narration, and music.
Comments: This DOS-based Bible program provides not only the standard Bible text but also multimedia presentations of the Bible that include graphical images of Bible events, music, and narration. The program does require a VGA graphics card in order to display the full-color images, but no CD-ROM or other specialized equipment is required.

ONESIMUS
Ark Multimedia Publishing
3323 W. Mercury Blvd.
Hampton VA 23666   (804) 838-2807

System requirements: IBM-PC or compatible.
Comments: This game is based on the life and times of Onesimus, Philemon's slave.

QUEST OF THE SCROLL SCHOLAR
Ark Multimedia Publishing
3323 W. Mercury Blvd.
Hampton VA 23666   (804) 838-2807

System requirements: IBM-PC or compatible.
Comments: This game emphasizes learning to identify Bible characters.

SPIRITUAL WARFARE
Wisdom Tree Software   (800) 77-BIBLE
2700 E. Imperial Highway, Bldg. A   (714) 528-3456
Brea CA 92621   (714) 961-1890 FAX

System requirements: IBM-PC or compatible.
Comments: This game is based on the theme of the Lord's soldier.

WHERE IN THE WORLD IS AMAZ'N BLAZ'N?
Navpress Software   (800) 366-7788
P.O. Box 35006   (719) 260-0404
Colorado Springs CO 80935   (719) 598-0749 FAX

System requirements: IBM-PC or compatible.
Comments: This program provides a collection of games based on the Old Testament character, Joseph.